UNSEND

UNSEND

EMAIL, TEXT, AND SOCIAL MEDIA
DISASTERS...AND HOW TO AVOID THEM

Kent Alan Robinson, Ph.D., MBA

TABLE OF CONTENTS

For Kelly, Casey, Lauren, and Mia; my all.

If history were taught in the form of stories, it would never be forgotten.

RUDYARD KIPLING

INTRODUCTION

In the Beginning

I n 1971, Ray Tomlinson, a defense department contractor working for the Advanced Research Projects Agency Network (ARPANET), a precursor of the Internet, sent the first email using the "@" symbol to connect a user's name to their mailbox. It was sent from one Digital Equipment Corporation (DEC) computer to another DEC computer sitting side-by-side on the same desk. By the mid-1980s, email was widely used among academicians, military personnel, and government employees. However, emails could only be sent on networks running the same software.

The first Internet Service Provider (ISP) was started by The World in 1989 to provide direct access to the

Internet versus the more restrictive access provided by CompuServe, The Source, and others. Nathaniel Borenstein wrote a program called Multipurpose Internet Mail Extension (MIME) in 1992, which allowed attachments to be sent by email. America Online (AOL) provided Internet access and email for almost half of all U.S. homes in 1997 for a fee of $19.95 per month. Hotmail, one of the first free web-based email services, was launched in 1996 and AOL gradually went into decline. These technologies paved the way for other forms of electronic communication.

By 2013, according to the Radicati Group, there were 929 million business email accounts worldwide. One hundred thirty-eight billion business emails will be sent every day by 2017. It's fair to presume the content in some of those 40,000,000,000,000 business emails sent annually will prove problematic.

Shifting Attitudes
As technology has changed and the uses of electronic communication have multiplied, attitudes have changed toward how that technology should be used as well. An example of these changing attitudes is seen in the evolving policies of the U.S. State

Department wrestling with how to handle what was then called electronic mail. Starting in 1995, their electronic mail policy required emails be preserved as paper copies. However, the policy did not require saving every message. It was left to individuals to decide which emails concerned government activity and should be saved, and which did not and could be deleted.

When Colin Powell served as Secretary of State from 2001 to 2005, he used a private email account to conduct official business and did not archive any emails from his time in office. Four years later, in October 2009, a State Department policy update required that emails sent by government employees using private email accounts like Yahoo or Gmail be archived on government servers.

A furor played out on the front pages of the nation's newspapers for months when it was revealed in February 2015 that Hillary Clinton used a private email account to conduct official business while Secretary of State from 2009 to 2013. Her use of a private email account meant only those emails sent to State Department employees would be archived, and allowed for deletion of selected emails. After an investigation, attorneys from the Department of

Justice (DOJ) wrote in September 2015, "There is no question that former Secretary Clinton had authority to delete personal emails without agency supervision; she appropriately could have done so even if she were working on a government server." A separate investigation by the State Department Inspector General in May 2016 found "longstanding, systemic weaknesses" in the State Department's communications and record keeping that "go well beyond the tenure of any one Secretary of State." A third investigation concluding in July 2016 found no wrongdoing, but FBI Director James Comey stated at a press conference, "Although we did not find clear evidence that Secretary Clinton or her colleagues intended to violate laws governing the handling of classified information, there is evidence that they were extremely careless in their handling of very sensitive, highly classified information." When John Kerry became Secretary of State in 2013, all of his emails using his government email account were automatically archived.

Reply All

Schools once had business correspondence courses to teach the proper salutation, body, and closing of a business letter. The instantaneous nature of electronic communication now creates a spontaneous conversation versus more formal letter writing with time delays of days or weeks. The salutation is not "Dear Mr. Smith," it's simply the recipient's first name or no name, as if talking with the person face-to-face.

A sales manager in the 1980s would have informed his field representatives throughout the nation of a price increase by letter. No rep would have taken the time to write a reply, make copies for all the other reps, address the envelopes, stamp, and mail them. With email, every rep can hit "Reply All" and immediately communicate how the price increase might impact their sales. What once would have been one letter now becomes an email chain with dozens of contributors.

Let Me Tell You a Story

In September 2013, just thirty-five seconds short of landing to refuel, a medical transport helicopter crashed due to lack of fuel, killing the pilot, the patient, and two medical personnel. The thirty-two-year-old Army veteran pilot had three separate protocol-mandated fuel checks before starting the flight, including being verbally asked by ground control to check his fuel gauge immediately before takeoff. Still, he did not realize that he was short of fuel until after the first leg of his trip.

The National Transportation Safety Board (NTSB) determined that distraction from twenty-two text messages and fifty phone calls made and received on the pilot's personal cellphone during the preflight inspections and while piloting the helicopter caused the crash. The new NTSB recommendations resulting from the crash investigation were: A-13-7, A-13-8, A-13-9, A-13-10, A-13-11, A-13-12, A-13-13, A-13-14, A-13-15; and reiterated existing rules A-06-14, A-09-7, and A-09-88.

But it's the story, not the rules, that impacts hearts and minds, leaving a lasting impression that hopefully changes behavior. In an air crash, the black box records airspeed, cockpit conversations, and other data needed to reconstruct what triggered the crash. In corporate America, emails, text messages, and social media serve the same function.

The helicopter crash and electronic communication disasters have several common themes:

1. Both the pilot and the writers of electronic communication work independently without direct supervision.
2. Well-trained individuals become bored and complacent leading to costly mistakes.
3. Protocols and instructions can be ignored or violated.
4. They are 100 percent preventable.

Analysis Leads to Safety

In 1926, the precursor to the NTSB was formed to analyze aviation crashes. Since that time, over 132,000 accidents have been analyzed and over 13,000 recommendations made to the FAA. Understanding why a plane crashed and how to prevent future crashes has gradually taught us how to fly planes more safely. Worldwide in 1970, 320 million passengers flew with 1,500 fatalities. In 2012, 2.9 billion passengers flew with 480 fatalities. Flying became 28-fold safer in 42 years, saving 13,000 lives in 2012 alone.

Attributing a bad corporate outcome to technology is like attributing a plane crash to gravity. Gravity is the constant force that pulls a plane from the sky back to Earth, but what exactly went wrong and why? In the case of emails, texts, and social media, it's always user error. Analyzing the wreckage for the root cause should provide instruction in avoidance of future catastrophes.

The electronic communication disasters retold here offer lessons that are applicable to every industry at every level. The emails, texts, and posts that wreaked havoc on people's careers were written by credit analysts, engineers, directors, attorneys, CEOs, and the U.S. Surgeon General. The point is not to say, "Lord, what fools these mortals be." To the contrary, they were all experienced, highly educated professionals who were ensnared by electronic communication. The intent is to learn from their mistakes and avoid their fate.

The Medium Shapes the Message

Electronic communication has not changed the fundamental nature of business, but it has changed how others can view the internal decision-making processes of a corporation. Corporate emails, texts, and posts reveal the considerations, deliberations, hopes, and fears of the individuals involved in making decisions; all archived for later searches by date, keyword, sender, and recipient. Using only a tiny fraction of the total sent, the media can select messages to cobble together their desired narrative. Law enforcement agencies only need one email, text, or post to open an investigation.

Contemporary corporate structure includes compliance officers, risk managers, and multiple levels of review for many corporate documents. Numerous people in different departments endlessly review annual reports, ad campaigns, and press releases. Not so with electronic communication.

Anything and everything goes into emails and texts: links to Internet sites, cartoons, emoticons, quotes under the signature block, large, **bold**, CAPITALIZED fonts for emphasis, and all with no managerial oversight. There is no committee crafting a text for days and then running it past Legal for a final review. No one is reviewing the vast majority of the billions of emails sent every day. This lack of review mandates that individuals monitor their own postings, their own responses, or whether they should reply at all.

There are functions allowing a sender to know if their text was received and if their email was opened. Unfortunately there is no Unsend function. There is no button that retrieves a toxic message *after* it has been read, erases all memory of it, and eradicates all copies. To the sender's detriment, the speed of electronic communication only amplifies the number of people who read their offending words.

The Power of One

Think of the powerful feelings evoked by the picture of Marines raising the American flag at Iwo Jima, or the emotional response of seeing the American flag flying over the rubble of the World Trade Center after 9/11. A single employee, with one message, can succinctly capture the essence of a corporation the same way an iconic photograph captures a moment. Unfortunately, it is usually the negative messages that are published or used in lawsuits.

Most people do not see their words as power. The examples in this book give readers pause to think about the ramifications of their words and the impact they may have on an organization or their own career; time for the writer of an electronic communication to recall a story that is similar to their situation and choose their words with care.

In the wreckage of an electronic communication disaster, the employee usually loses their job, may be investigated, and occasionally is prosecuted. Most companies survive, albeit oftentimes with a multibillion-dollar fine, damage to their reputation, loss of key personnel, and distraction from execution of their mission. The company remains; the employee who wrote the career-destroying message leaves.

The numerous examples of devastating emails, texts, and posts leaked to the public or used in an investigation serve as a stark reminder that with electronic communication, what one writes in a moment, eternity will not erase.

GONE, BUT NOT FORGOTTEN

Facing the Abyss

In autumn 2001, the nation's sixth largest corporation, Enron, was teetering on the financial precipice. An acute lack of cash flow and rating agencies taking steps to lower Enron's credit to junk status made continuing daily operations a precarious proposition. The death knell sounded when some of the sham partnerships, designed to hide losses and approved by the corporation's accounting firm Arthur Andersen, began unraveling. Losses of over one billion dollars, which had been hidden for the previous two years, were publicly announced, pummeling their share price. Enron filed for bankruptcy on December 2, 2001.

Arthur Andersen, the nation's largest accounting firm at that time, was keenly aware that a crisis for Enron was a crisis for Andersen, perhaps even of such magnitude as to take it down as well. In the previous two and a half years, Andersen had paid just over one-third of a billion dollars in Security Exchange Commission (SEC) fines and settlements in two shareholders' lawsuits for facilitating multiyear, multibillion-dollar accounting frauds. Andersen was currently operating under a cease and desist order from engaging in similar activities. Enron looked like a similar activity.

Andersen was operating in crisis mode. In both the previous shareholder lawsuits and the SEC settlements, Andersen was required to provide the Department of Justice with emails and other internal documents, which resulted in their conviction. They were determined not to retain any Enron emails or records the DOJ could subpoena except those required to be saved by Andersen's own internal document-destruction policy.

Michael Odom, a Practice Director at Andersen involved with the Enron account, gave a presentation on Andersen's document-destruction policy to a room full of audit managers on October 10, 2001 that was videotaped. He stated that all documents not essential for an audit: handwritten notes, emails, and minutes of meetings, should be promptly destroyed. He went on to say that after legal action was taken, nothing else could be destroyed. "If it's destroyed in the course of the normal policy and litigation is filed the next day, that's great, you know, because we've followed our own policy and whatever there was of interest to somebody is gone and irretrievable." The reason Andersen thought it was a good idea to videotape a presentation on destroying evidence, but not destroy that videotape, is unclear.

Thirteen days after the videotaped meeting, the SEC announced that an inquiry, not an investigation, had been opened concerning Enron. David Duncan, the Andersen partner who managed the Enron account, held another meeting to remind everyone of Andersen's document-destruction policy. The SEC inquiry kicked the document-destruction process into overdrive. Over a ton of documents were shredded using a mobile truck parked on the street outside Andersen's downtown Houston office, and over 30,000 emails were deleted. The shredding and deletions did not stop until the SEC served

Andersen with a subpoena a month and a half later, on November 30, 2001.

In June 2002, Andersen was convicted of obstruction of justice and fined $500,000, the maximum amount allowed by law, for destroying Enron-related documents. Andersen was now a convicted felon and could not file audits with the SEC on behalf of clients, which put the company out of business.

Sarbanes Oxley

After Enron, and more than 700 other documented corporate accounting scandals that occurred in the 1990s, there was national outrage over the CEOs and members of senior management who stole hundreds of millions of dollars from public companies while investors lost billions and employees lost their jobs. There was no national outrage demanding all corporate emails be archived. The demand was for reform of corporate governance to prevent the accounting abuses from recurring.

In July 2002, just eight months after Enron's bankruptcy, President George W. Bush signed into law the "Public Company Accounting Reform and

Investor Protection Act," known as Sarbanes Oxley. The new legislation only tangentially dealt with emails by mandating that any records that might be needed in a whistleblower lawsuit be archived, effectively necessitating that all corporate electronic correspondence be retained.

Sarbanes Oxley only applies to U.S.-registered, publicly traded corporations, so federal, state, and municipal agencies, foreign corporations such as BMW and Mercedes, and private corporations are exempt from compliance. However, exemption from compliance under Sarbanes Oxley is not exemption from the ramifications of not archiving emails.

Keep Your Federal Laws Off Our Federal Agency

Members of Congress requested that the U.S. Treasury Inspector General for Tax Administration audit the IRS due to complaints by conservative political groups they were being targeted for extreme delays in receiving IRS tax-exempt status from the Cincinnati branch. The final report of the audit, released in May 2013, determined that this branch of the IRS specifically targeted groups with "Tea

Party" and "Patriot" in their names by requesting unnecessary information and delaying processing of applications. The report determined that "ineffective management" allowed these criteria to be developed and kept in place for more than eighteen months, resulting in substantial delays in processing.

Lost and Found

The report prompted two Republican-chaired House committees to open IRS investigations. Lois Lerner, the IRS Director of Tax-Exempt Organizations, was subpoenaed and promptly retired. However, she was still required to appear before the Congressional committees in March 2014, where she declined to answer questions. The committees also wanted to examine the emails between Lerner and the Cincinnati branch, but were told by the IRS in June 2014 that it had lost about two years' worth of emails when Lerner's computer crashed in mid-2011. A month later, IRS management said that some of the missing emails might be found on backup tapes that were recycled several years previously. The recycling was supposed to destroy the emails but might not have. IRS Deputy Associate Chief Counsel Thomas Kane testified: "There is an issue as to whether or not…all of the backup recovery tapes were destroyed on the six-month retention schedule."

Somehow, on July 30, 2014, newly discovered emails surfaced between Lerner and a friend or family member from Lerner's vacation in the United Kingdom.

Lerner: "Overheard some ladies talking about America today. According to them we've bankrupted ourselves and at [*sic*, are] through. We'll never be able to pay off our debt and are going down the tubes."

Friend: "Well, you should hear the whacko wing of the GOP…The right-wing radio shows are scary to listen to."

Lerner: "Great. Maybe we are through if there are that many [expletive]."

Friend: "And I'm talking about the hosts of the shows. The callers are rabid."

Lerner: "So we don't need to worry about alien teR-rorists (*sic*). It's our own crazies that will take us down."

The Republican House Ways and Means Chairman Dave Camp said the exchange "directly demonstrates Ms. Lerner's deep animus towards conservatives" and that her "mistreatment of conservative groups was driven by her personal hostility toward conservatives."

A year after the emails from Lerner's vacation surfaced, the Treasury Inspector General testified that 422 backup tapes containing emails from Lerner covering the dates subpoenaed by Congress were erased at the same time she was testifying before Congress. The Inspector General added that there was no evidence the destruction of backup tapes containing the emails subpoenaed by Congress was part of a cover up.

"...Lost, Deleted, or Destroyed"

Takeda, Asia's largest pharmaceutical manufacturer, is not publicly traded in the United States and, therefore, is not under the purview of Sarbanes Oxley.

Takeda was sued in Lafayette, Louisiana in February 2014 over allegations that researchers suppressed data about its diabetes drug, Actos, and misled the FDA about its carcinogenic risks. Revenue from Actos was $4.5 billion in 2011 and accounted for slightly over one-quarter of Takeda's gross revenue.

Takeda officials admitted they could not find emails and other documents pertaining to Actos from forty-six current and former employees involved in the research, development, and marketing of the drug. Some emails were deleted after executives specifically instructed employees not to delete communications or files relating to Actos. Before the trial began, U.S. District Judge Rebecca Doherty allowed the jury to hear that Takeda had intentionally destroyed evidence relating to Actos and to presume it would have had a negative impact. She wrote in January 2014 that the breadth of the files that had been "lost, deleted, or destroyed is, in and of itself, disturbing."

In April 2014, after a two-month trial, the jury deliberated for only four hours and awarded the plaintiffs $9 billion, over half the $16 billion Actos had generated since its launch fifteen years earlier in 1999. Shares of Takeda dropped by over 5 percent on the Tokyo Stock

Exchange the day the judgment was announced. It was the seventh-largest jury award in U.S. history.

...and how to avoid them

Josef Djugashvili changed his name to Joseph Stalin, meaning "man of steel" in Russian. Stalin altered official photographs by deleting pictures of rivals he had eliminated. History was once rewritten by the victors. Now we write our own immutable histories with every email, tweet, and post. Electronic communication has transmuted conversations into durable and accessible records. Revisionist history has gone the way of the phone booth.

Emails are viewed as an essential historical record of an organization, and their deletion carries a presumption of guilt. A record that cannot be expunged must be created with care or not created at all.

LINE UPON LINE

Standard and Poor's (S&P)

The Standard and Poor's 500 stock market index is the best-known S&P product. However, another division of the company rates corporate bonds. Bonds are money that a corporation has borrowed from investors at a set interest rate for a specified number of years.

In much the same way Experian, Equifax, and TransUnion use payment history, amount of debt owed, and credit history to assign a FICO score for individuals, S&P and its two largest competitors, Moody's and Fitch, assign credit ratings to bonds. The FICO score runs from 850, for people most likely to pay their debts, down to 300 for those most likely to default. For bonds, the highest rating is AAA and the lowest is CCC.

Similar to Experian, Equifax, and TransUnion, bonds are given similar, and oftentimes identical ratings by S&P, Moody's, and Fitch. Investment-grade bonds are AAA through BBB and non – investment grade (junk bonds) are BB through CCC.

Pension funds, insurance companies, federally insured banks, and federally insured credit unions purchase investment-grade bonds to minimize their risk of loss. By law, credit unions can only buy AAA or AA bonds.

Pay to Play

Although the goal of both individual and commercial credit rating agencies is to determine the likelihood of a debt being repaid, individuals pay nothing to have their creditworthiness rated. S&P, Moody's, and Fitch charge a fee for each bond that is rated, which is paid by the entity whose bond is being rated. This creates a huge potential conflict of interest because the higher the bond rating, the more money the client makes through lower interest payments. Additionally, the three rating agencies compete for clients, so looser rating standards than your competitors (i.e., higher ratings than warranted) would mean both the client and the rating company would make more money.

S&P repeatedly acknowledged this potential conflict of interest and, over the course of years, publicly reaffirmed its commitment to independent ratings free from competitive pressures. Examples of public statements made by S&P were:

- The 2004 S&P Code of Practices and Procedures stated: "[Our] mission has always remained the same, to provide objective, independent information not compromised by conflicts of interest."
- The 2005 S&P Code of Conduct read: "[S&P] endeavors to conduct rating and surveillance in a manner that is transparent and credible and that also ensures that the integrity and independence of such processes are not compromised by conflicts of interest."
- A 2006 S&P website posting stated: "It is the central tenet of S&P that the ratings decisions not be influenced by the fact that S&P receives fees from issuers."
- A 2007 S&P website posting stated: "One way for us to increase revenue would be to weaken

our criteria to ensure that we are selected as the rating agency. We do not engage in such behavior."

Faulty Construct

Fannie Mae and Freddie Mac are federally sponsored private enterprises that purchase and hold home mortgages originated by banks and mortgage brokers so those lenders can, in turn, make more home loans. In 1990, 80 percent of residential loans acquired by Fannie and Freddie were prime loans, meaning a healthy down payment and a well-documented ability by borrowers to make loan payments. But a 1992 federal housing bill aimed at increasing the level of national home ownership required that 30 percent of the mortgages purchased by Fannie and Freddie be subprime (loans to those with lower credit scores or lower incomes, and sometimes even to those lacking documentation or verification of income). The subprime loan requirement was raised over the next sixteen years until it stood at 56 percent in 2008 when both Fannie and Freddie collapsed at the height of the housing crisis.

Concurrent to the increased requirements to provide subprime lending, securitization of home loans by the private sector also increased the financing available for home buyers. Securitization is the pooling of various types of debt, in this case residential mortgages, and selling that pool of debt as bonds, primarily to institutional investors such as insurance companies and banks. These bundles of debt, known as Residential Mortgage-Backed Securities (RMBSs), were often valued in the hundreds of millions of dollars and required an investment-grade rating by a commercial rating agency, such as S&P, before banks, credits unions, and other investors could buy them. The chief concern of banks and credit unions was preservation of capital, insuring they got their money back. In 1990, few home loans were securitized; by 2007, almost all were. Revenue from rating mortgage-backed securities at both Moody's and S&P nearly quadrupled from 2002 through 2007.

The combination of federal policies increasing the number of home buyers, many with poorer credit, coupled with securitization, massively increased funding available to home buyers. More money and more buyers created a demand for homes with predictable results. Nationwide, home prices more than doubled from 1997 through 2006.

Stem of the Martini Glass

Collateralized Debt Obligations (CDOs) are ways to slice an RMBS based upon risk. Portions with a higher risk of default have higher interest rates. There could be multiple CDOs derived from a single RMBS. The RMBS is the stem of the martini glass supporting the CDO. If the underlying RMBS fails, so goes the CDO.

With computer algorithms doing the calculations, the mechanics of getting an RMBS rated are relatively straightforward. If Merrill Lynch had a bundle of home loans they wanted S&P to rate, they would email a spreadsheet containing the financial data on each individual home loan over to S&P to run through their rating algorithm and give Merrill Lynch a preliminary rating. The fee for this first look was approximately $15,000. If the preliminary rating S&P gave Merrill Lynch was too low (i.e., not investment-grade, as was required to be purchased by banks or credit unions), Merrill Lynch could add more collateral or shop that same mortgage package to Moody's or Fitch in hopes of obtaining a higher rating. Fees for providing a final rating for an RMBS or CDOs derived from an RMBS were roughly $150,000 and $750,000, respectively. If the investment bank did not purchase the final rating after receiving the initial rating, the S&P analyst had to fill out a "Lost Deal" report explaining why the deal was not closed.

Between September 2004 and October 2007, S&P rated almost 18,000 RMBSs and CDOs valued at over four trillion dollars, many of which were subprime. Unlike rating a traditional corporate bond, rating an RMBS placed S&P in the position of determining the ability of hundreds of thousands of individuals to collectively support the repayment of thousands of multimillion dollar bond pools.

Did S&P Intentionally Mislead Investors?

Historically, a corporate bond rated AAA by S&P had a 1:200 chance of defaulting. In 2006, federally insured financial intuitions lost billions of dollars shortly after purchasing bonds rated as investment-grade by S&P that should have rarely defaulted. A small sampling of the losses incurred is shown below:

Sample of subprime CDO losses cited in federal lawsuit

Institution	Bond rating	Amount	Loss	Months between purchase and loss
Citibank	AAA	$15 million	100%	6 months
WestCorp	AAA	$90 million	~95%	1 month
Eastern Finance CU	AAA	$50 million	100%	6 months
Citibank	A-BBB	$8 million	~95%	2 months
First Midwest	A	$8.8 million	~95%	12 months

In 1999, S&P calculated default probabilities for RMBSs using a historical database of 166,000 individual prime home loans. Three years later, S&P had increased that database to 642,000 individual home loans, many subprime, which more accurately reflected the composition of the RMBSs and CDOs they were rating. S&P planned to start using its updated 642,000-mortgage model for rating RMBSs in 2004. However, an S&P analyst warned executives in a May 2004 email that they were losing business because the updated ratings model was more conservative (gave lower ratings) than Moody's and Fitch.

Analyst: "We just lost a huge Mizuho [mortgage-backed] deal to Moody's due to a huge difference in the required credit support level. This is so significant that it could have an impact on future deals."

S&P did not use the new database and continued to rate subprime RMBSs using the old 166,000-mortgage model derived from prime home loans.

Previously, when S&P, Moody's, and Fitch were sued by investors who had lost money relying on their ratings, the agencies claimed their ratings reflected opinions that were protected under the First Amendment. The DOJ claimed S&P intentionally delayed using the more accurate model, which generated lower credit ratings in order to maintain market share. Knowingly misrating the bonds as investment grade when S&P knew the bonds should have been rated as junk was not merely stating an opinion, but constituted fraud. The misrated bonds caused losses for the federally insured banks and the credit unions that purchased them.

Burning Down the Market

In March 2007, a meeting was held of S&P's CDO analysts to discuss the deteriorating residential market. In that meeting, the analysts were told investment bankers had huge inventories of subprime RMBSs they were eager to sell before the market collapsed, which everyone saw as eminent. The rush to beat a collapse would also lead to a spike in rating business. The analysts were told to trust the S&P ratings model derived from the prime home loans, comply with the criteria, and give higher ratings. During that meeting, one CDO analyst sent an instant message to another analyst.

Analyst: "a meeting to discuss the blow up of the resi[dential] market."

Within seconds, the eleven-word IM created a permanent, electronic record of the content of the meeting and one analyst's reaction.

An IM exchange from two other analysts at the same meeting captured the content and gave an analysis.

Analyst 1: "we got the gist of it"
Analyst 2: "that means market will crash...deals will rush in before they take further loss"
Analyst 1: "yes"
Analyst 2: "that means we will see grumpy analyst sand (*sic*) grumpy bankers and a grumpy [Managing Director in Global CDO]"

Analyst 1: "I'm grympy (*sic*) anyway"
Analyst 2: "but then we should not push the criteria but we give in anyway ahahhahaha"

On March 12, 2007, an analyst used the more accurate 642,000-mortgage rating model containing the subprime data to rate some of the RMBSs that S&P had previously rated using the 166,000-mortgage model derived primarily from prime mortgages. His analysis showed a high risk of downgrade, which he emailed to an executive.

Executive: "Wow, these deals are in huge trouble."

One week after conducting the analysis showing the potential for huge losses on the bonds S&P had rated, the same analyst sent an email to his colleagues.

Analyst: "With apologies to David Byrne [lead singer of 1980s band Talking Heads]...here's my version of "Burning Down the House":

Watch out
Housing market went softer
Cooling down

Strong market is now much weaker
Subprime is boiling over
Bringing down the house

Hold tight
CDO biz — has bother
Leveraged CDOs they were after
Going — all the way down, with
Subprime mortgages

Own it
Hey you need a downgrade now
Free-mont [name of a subprime CDO]
Two-thousand-and-six-vintage
Bringing down the house."

Two minutes later he followed up with another email.

Analyst: "For obvious, professional reasons please do not forward this song. If you are interested, I can sing it in your cube ;-)."

Two days later, he sent out another email with a video of himself singing and dancing the first verse of his new lyrics to "Burning Down the House" while other analysts laughed in the background. Although only identified as "Analyst D" in the lawsuit, the original email circulated at S&P clearly displayed his name. It's difficult to imagine the emails furthered his career.

A month after that meeting, S&P learned of more bad news regarding the performance of the subprime RMBSs they had rated. Their response was large-scale downgrades, meaning the initial ratings were lowered. An IM exchange between two CDO analysts reflected their belief that S&P's rating model was underestimating the credit risk.

Analyst 1: "btw that deal is ridiculous"
Analyst 2: "I know right...model def[initely] does not capture half of the risk"
Analyst 1: "We should not be rating it"
Analyst 2: "we rate every deal...it could be structured by cows and we would rate it"
Analyst 1: "but there's a lot of risk associated with it — I personally don't feel comfy signing off as a committee member"

From March through June 2007, as predicted in its earlier meeting, S&P booked record profits by rating RMBSs and CDOs for investment bankers.

An investment banking client asked a recently hired S&P analyst how things were going via email in July 2007.

Investment banker: "How's the new job?"

Analyst: "Job's going great. Aside from the fact that the MBS [mortgage-backed securities] world is crashing, investors and the media hate us, and we are all running around trying to save face...no complaints."

Two days later the analyst continued the email string.

Analyst: "The fact is, there was a lot of internal pressure in S&P to downgrade lots of deals earlier on before this thing started blowing up. But the leadership was concerned of p*ssing off too many clients and jumping the gun ahead of Fitch and Moody's."

Investment banker: "I mean come on, we pay you to rate our deals, and the better the rating the more money we make?!?! Whats (*sic*) up with that? How are you possibly supposed to be impartial?????"

Analyst: "Nah. I'll admit it. We dropped the ball on this one. But you think it's bad now, wait 'till next week (hint, hint)"

The next day, S&P announced more downgrades of numerous subprime RMBSs and CDOs from investment grade to junk, which resulted in a massive price drop due to the greater risk of default. Banks and credit unions were now forced to sell the downgraded bonds because they were no longer investment-grade. This flooded the market and further lowered bond prices.

Five Years and Twenty Million Emails Later

In February 2013, U.S. Attorney General Eric Holder announced a $5 billion lawsuit against S&P. The Department of Justice based its lawsuit upon S&P's website postings, emails, employees' texts, and other documents. The DOJ alleged S&P deceived investors by intentionally misrating bonds backed by subprime mortgages. Line upon line, the electronic communications written by S&P's own employees were used to build the federal lawsuit against S&P. Building the case was a time-consuming and arduous undertaking for the DOJ, requiring twenty-three attorneys to review twenty million S&P emails over the course of five years.

Why Not Sue Moody's and Fitch?

The Senate Permanent Subcommittee on Investigations found that in 2006, 93 percent of all the subprime mortgage-backed securities rated AAA by S&P, Moody's, and Fitch, were later down-graded to junk status. If all three rating firms did the same catastrophically poor job of rating sub-prime mortgage-backed securities, why did the DOJ choose to prosecute S&P rather than Moody's or Fitch?

The only difference seemed to be that Moody's and Fitch lacked texts and emails such as, "we rate every deal...it could be structured by cows and we would rate it" and the "Burning Down the House" parody. At the press conference announcing the lawsuit against S&P, Attorney General Holder said, "...this conduct is egregious."

The "Burning Down the House" parody and dancing video did not appear in the media until they were reported as part of the DOJ lawsuit. It appears that someone forwarded an email to the DOJ, triggering the investigation. The egregious emails gave the DOJ so much leverage that S&P could not risk going before a jury and could only hope to negotiate the best settlement possible.

Providing the Rope for Their Own Hanging

Broadly, the public documents used in the DOJ lawsuit stated that S&P's ratings would always be fair and never swayed by wanting to generate more fees. The internal documents allegedly showed their ratings were not fair and were swayed by wanting to generate more fees. The number and type of documents cited in the DOJ lawsuit against S&P were:

Public Documents Used in the DOJ Lawsuit

Website postings:	26
Annual reports:	8
Press releases:	7
S&P publications:	3
Senate Hearings on S&P:	2
House of Representatives hearing:	1

Wall Street Journal Op/Ed, by S&P:	1
Investors' teleconference:	1
Letter to the SEC by S&P:	1

Internal Documents Used in the DOJ Lawsuit

Total number of emails reviewed:	20,000,000
Emails cited in lawsuit:	42
Emails reviewed, but not used:	19, 999,958
Average length per email:	48 words
Memoranda and reports:	30
Meeting agendas and minutes:	10
PowerPoint presentations:	5
Rating algorithms:	3
Instant messages:	2
Phone calls:	1
Strategic Plan:	1
Video:	1

The DOJ's 119-page lawsuit cited specific emails, instant messages, and other internal documents. Of S&P's 6,000 employees, only twenty, or fewer than one half of 1 percent of S&P's total employees, were cited in the lawsuit. Some were cited by name and others only by title such as "Sr. Manager A." The S&P emails were extraordinary in how ordinary they were. The emails were usually two to four sentences in length, contained misspellings and grammatical errors, and had questions ending with "????". In short, they were like the emails found at every company in America.

Talk Is Not Cheap

In February 2015, two years after the DOJ brought suit against S&P and seven years after opening the investigation, a settlement was reached for $1.37 billion, which represented about four months of S&P's earnings. S&P did not admit wrongdoing as part of the settlement. The federally insured institutions that lost money received half of the proceeds with the remainder going to twenty states and the District of Columbia.

Twenty-six of the fifty pieces of public evidence used by the DOJ came from S&P's own website. The S&P site in 2016 has a more cautious, guarded tone and extensively uses the words "may" and "opinion" regarding their ratings. "Credit ratings are opinions about credit risk published by a rating agency. They express opinions...Credit ratings are also opinions about the credit quality of an issue, such as a bond or other debt obligation, and the relative likelihood that it may default."

...and how to avoid them

The S&P debacle contains lessons that are applicable to both corporations and individuals.

Corporations

The cynical flippancy shown in the analysts' texts and emails reflected a profound lack of respect for management as it was an open secret the rating model analysts were forced to use was inherently flawed in favor of S&P. Management traded its moral authority for immediate fees. Employees were participants in a charade that enriched those possessing knowledge while inflicting catastrophic losses on those dependent on analysts for accurate information. Pursuing perceived self-interests at the expense of clients was to the detriment of both.

People act in ways to maximize their self-interest within a company, so create incentives that align employee's objectives with the organization's mission statement. Reward compliance with core values as much as profitability, especially in the face of competitive pressures. S&P's mission statement "to provide objective, independent information not compromised by conflicts of interest" was meaningless without a metric that impacted year-end bonuses. Both management and analysts profited in year-end bonuses by using the inaccurate rating model.

Employees

Juries have difficulty understanding complex subjects like default risk, but they immediately understand an employee entertaining coworkers by making sport of millions of Americans losing their homes. The insensitive, sarcastic emails later proved devastating to S&P. An egregious email cannot be minimized later. Perfection in one's job is not required, but a perception of being sincere and diligent is.

Keep confidential company information confidential. When asked how things are going by someone outside the company, do not divulge information that is not already publicly disclosed. The S&P analyst who emailed a client, "But you think it's bad now, wait 'til next week (hint, hint)," disclosed confidential, market-moving information.

S&P argued that the DOJ cherry-picked the most incriminating emails, which is true, but S&P employees wrote all of the emails volitionally. Of the twenty million emails read by the DOJ, only forty-two, or roughly one in 500,000 of the total emails, were used in the lawsuit. In a company of three, every employee recognizes that their actions reflect upon the organization. For larger companies, employees may lose that sense of connection. No matter the size of the company or one's position within it, the content of every email, text, or social media posting has the potential for devastating consequences.

One Hundred Times Bigger than Enron

The ratings firms were not the only industry complicit in the housing crisis. Five years after Sarbanes Oxley was passed to prevent accounting fraud, the nation suffered from the ineffectiveness of this legislation. While investors and lenders lost about $90 billion in Enron, the housing crisis was estimated to have cost investors, lenders, and taxpayers at least $9 trillion. Once again, the pursuit of fees and growth prevailed over the common good and, ultimately, the corporation's best interests.

Hero to Zero

In 2006, Citigroup had assets of $1.9 trillion, earnings of over $21 billion, and 373,000 employees in over 100 countries around the world. It boasted of being the only U.S.-based bank with a truly global reach. One year later, earnings were down by 83 percent. Citigroup's 2007 annual report stated the drop in earnings was caused by "…write-downs related to subprime CDOs." These losses occurred in spite of the fact that revenue in other areas of the bank increased by roughly 20 percent. Belatedly, the annual report went on to state, "…we are aggressively building a new risk management culture." Despite its efforts, Citigroup lost $27.7 billion, fired 52,000 employees, and cut dividends by 40 percent the following year. Transcripts from the Financial Crisis Inquiry Commission's hearing on subprime lending revealed the decisions leading to Citigroup's losses and concluded they were preventable had Citigroup followed the advice given in one employee's emails.

Lining up the Dominoes

At its peak in 2006, there were approximately 1,600 non-Citigroup mortgage brokers throughout the country who originated home loans using Citigroup's underwriting criteria, which included: employment verification, income documentation, and debt-to-income ratio. These individual home loans were bundled into pools ranging in size from $20 million to $400 million. The originating mortgage brokers guaranteed Citigroup that 95 percent of the pool met Citigroup's underwriting criteria or they would buy back the entire pool.

Citigroup's Quality Assurance department was staffed with 220 mortgage underwriters who would randomly select individual home loans from a pool to ensure they met Citigroup's criteria. The annual dollar amount of residential mortgages that passed through Citigroup exceeded $90 billion, but only a fraction was analyzed for compliance. Once a pool of home loans had passed Citigroup's internal Quality Assurance department, the majority were sold to Fannie Mae or Freddie Mac who, in turn, were given legally binding warrantees by Citigroup that 95 percent of the package conformed to Citigroup's underwriting standards or Citigroup would buy back the entire pool.

Citigroup's market share of mortgage originations had been rapidly increasing. Citigroup was ranked thirteenth industry-wide in residential mortgage origination in 2001, sixth in 2005, and third in 2006. It was announced that greater growth was anticipated in

2007. Most of the growth was expected to come from subprime mortgages, which Citigroup referred to as nonprime. In July 2006, Bill Beckman, President of Citifinancial Mortgage, said, "…increased nonprime production is the biggest opportunity."

Thumbing Their Nose at Danger

Richard Bowen, C.P.A., was the Sr. Vice President and Chief Underwriter of Citifinancial Mortgage from 2002 to 2006. His job was to ensure that the mortgage pools purchased met Citigroup's credit standards, but he lacked authorization to block the purchase of any mortgage pools. By mid-2006, Bowen discovered that over 60 percent of the mortgages purchased and subsequently sold by Citigroup to Fannie or Freddie were defective by not meeting credit guidelines. This meant investors could force Citigroup to repurchase billions of dollars worth of defective subprime mortgages, posing a huge risk to shareholders. Despite Bowen's warnings of this potential liability in emails, weekly reports, and discussions, the defective mortgage rate increased during 2007 to over 80 percent.

As credit quality deteriorated, Citigroup found ways around acknowledging the problem in order to maintain growth. According to Bowen's testimony, in the third quarter of 2006, the Chief Risk Officer started changing many of the underwriting decisions on individual home loans from "Turn down" to "Approve." This was done either personally by the Chief Risk Officer, or by directing the underwriters to change their ratings. The falsified higher approval rate was then used to justify the purchase of the defective mortgage pool.

In one pool of over $300 million in subprime loans, the underwriters labeled 716 home loans as "Turn down." The Chief Risk Officer personally changed 260 loans to "Approve." The pool was purchased while Bowen was on vacation.

"URGENT — READ IMMEDIATELY — FINANCIAL ISSUES"

After sending numerous emails to multiple levels of management detailing the subprime mortgage situation, on Saturday, November 3, 2007, Bowen sent an email to the following Citigroup executives:

- Robert Rubin, Chairman of Executive Committee
- David Bushnell, Senior Risk Officer
- Gary Crittenden, Chief Financial Officer
- Bonnie Howard, Chief Auditor

The subject line of the email read: "URGENT — READ IMMEDIATELY — FINANCIAL ISSUES." In his email, Bowen warned that 80 percent of the mortgages Citigroup was selling and guaranteeing to investors were defective.

Bowen: "I do not believe that our company has recognized the material financial losses inevitably associated with the above Citi liability. Please contact me. You need to know the details behind this. There are risks to the company."

Bowen requested that another division of Citigroup conduct an internal audit of the creditworthiness of the mortgage pools. He provided his cellphone number and asked to be called over the weekend. Neither a call nor a reply to his email was received. Bowen was demoted and later left the bank in January 2009 with a signed confidentiality agreement and a severance package of less than one million dollars.

Day of Reckoning

Unfortunately, the drastic lowering of lending standards seen at Citigroup was endemic throughout the home lending industry. Citigroup, J. P. Morgan, Wells Fargo, Bank of America, and Morgan Stanley collectively paid $127 billion in fines and lawsuit settlements relating to their home lending practices. Fannie Mae and Freddie Mac, the ultimate buyers or guarantors of $5 trillion in mortgage obligations, were taken over by the federal government in September 2008.

The collapse of the housing market fueled a recession that saw unemployment rise from 5 percent in 2007 to a peak of 10 percent in 2010. Foreclosures in the United States rose from 2.2 million homes in 2007 to 3.9 million homes in 2011.

"I Honestly — I Truly Do Not Remember."

Twenty-nine months after receiving the email from Bowen, Robert Rubin testified before the congressionally funded Financial Crisis Inquiry Commission. The chairman, Phil Angelides, asked Rubin to respond to Bowen's email.

Rubin replied, "Mr. Chairman, I do recollect this, and that — either I or somebody else — and I truly do not remember who, but either I or somebody else sent it to the appropriate people — I certainly don't remember today whether I knew at the time or not — I honestly — I truly do not remember."

In fairness to Rubin, he was appointed Chairman of the Executive Committee one day before receiving the email from Bowen and served in that capacity for only thirty-eight days between the resignation of Charles Prince and the hiring of Sir Win Bischoff. According to testimony from an executive at Rubin's level, it would not be uncommon to receive 1,000 texts and emails per day. In almost two and half years, it's possible to forget an individual email and the action taken on it.

Chairman Phil Angelides responded to Rubin's comment with, "If the excuse at the top was 'We didn't know,' that's a pretty poor excuse from people who are hauling down $10 million, $20 million, $30 million, or in Robert Rubin's case, $115 million." Rubin's pay for his decade of work at Citi was $126 million.

If They Did Not Know, Who Did?

Rubin's defense was to plead ignorance. But was it possible for a person outside the banking community to foresee the pending implosion in home prices? John Paulson, founder of the Paulson & Company hedge fund, talked to one of his analysts in early 2006 and said, "This is crazy," referring to home prices. He asked the analyst to determine if housing was a speculative bubble. Using publicly available data, the analyst found that housing prices from 2000 through 2005 had increased five times faster than the historic average. The data showed that each time housing prices sharply increased, prices eventually dropped below the historical average. Paulson was confident that he had identified a bubble and started a new fund to profit from what he perceived was the pending collapse in home prices.

Paulson took positions against subprime mortgages, making $15 billion in 2007. He personally made almost $4 billion, or a little over $10 million every day for one year. It was the largest payout in the history of financial markets for one year's profits

"Egregious Misconduct"

On July 14, 2014, seven years after Richard Bowen's email to Robert Rubin, Attorney General Eric Holder announced that Citigroup and the

Department of Justice had negotiated a $7 billion fine for what Holder described as "egregious misconduct" in Citigroup's pooling of subprime mortgages. "Despite the fact that Citigroup learned of serious and widespread defects among the increasingly risky loans they were securitizing, the bank and its employees concealed these defects. They misrepresented the facts, including the level of risk. They sold defective loans to countless investors, including federally insured financial institutions."

...and how to avoid them

Although subprime lending was the common denominator in both the S&P and Citigroup examples, it did not cause their problems. The change in subprime lending occurred gradually over the course of years and serve as a backdrop for the changes and competitive pressures facing every industry. The emails and texts recorded the systemic violations of guidelines intended to prevent the disasters that inevitably occurred.

A very limited number of people in key positions within Citigroup violated the safeguards and policies put in place specifically to prevent catastrophic losses. Had a few people at critical checkpoints insisted that mortgage originators maintain credit standards as contractually agreed upon, the $7 billion fine and the operating losses could have been avoided.

Direction and guidance from management and a person's immediate superior are usually followed. However, contributions from subordinates are easily minimized or ignored, especially if critical of management. If you ask, and are willing to listen, there is probably a person in your company who can provide timely counsel.

An email cannot be ignored. You may wish an email was not sent to you, because you learned what you did not want to know, but it must be acted upon because there is now a permanent record linking you to that information. Use email to your advantage and contact a manager in Finance, Legal, or Compliance or a member of the board of directors about egregious misconduct.

PANDORA'S BOX

A Gift?

The strengths of electronic communication are speed and accessibility. The weaknesses of electronic communication are speed and accessibility. Messages originally intended to remain private, much to the consternation of the sender, are routinely disinterred, sometimes years after they were originally sent. Like Pandora's box, they often unleash a torrent of misery: investigations, resignations, and high-profile firings. The release of electronic communication to the public broadly falls into three categories:

- Subpoenaed messages related to suspected illegal activities

- Leaks involving potentially illegal activities
- Leaks designed to make the sender look incompetent or disingenuous

Subpoenaed Messages Related to Suspected Illegal Activities

George Washington Bridge

The Port Authority (PA) of New York & New Jersey conceives, builds, and operates infrastructure critical to the New York/New Jersey trade region. Some of these facilities include the JFK and LaGuardia airports, the Lincoln and Holland tunnels, and the George Washington Bridge. As a bi-state agency, the governors of New York and New Jersey appoint its administrators. The PA receives no tax revenue. It generates revenue from tolls, user fees, fares, and rental income.

In February 2010, New Jersey Governor Chris Christie appointed William Baroni, then a Republican state senator, to the position of Deputy Executive Director of the PA. Later that year, Baroni appointed David Wildstein to be the PA's Director of Interstate Capital Projects.

"Time for Some Traffic Problems"

On Sunday, September 8, 2013, Wildstein called two George Washington Bridge officials and ordered them to close two of the three access lanes across the bridge from Fort Lee, New Jersey to northern Manhattan. No notice was given to police, emergency officials, or to New York officials within the PA. The lane closures triggered massive traffic jams for a week on the New Jersey side of the bridge. The closures were reported to be for a traffic pattern study, but later appeared to be political payback for the Democratic Mayor of Fort Lee Mark Sokolich, who refused to endorse Republican Governor Chris Christie.

The lanes were closed for five days before PA Executive Director Patrick Foye learned of them from a daily internal list of pending media inquiries and ordered the lanes reopened. In an email to other PA executives, which was leaked to the media, he said the lane closings had potentially endangered lives and violated state and federal law. Foye denounced the closures as "abusive" and pledged to investigate "how PA process was wrongfully subverted and the public interest damaged to say nothing of the credibility of this agency." He stated the lane closures were made without informing him, Port Authority police, the PA Traffic and Engineering division, Mayor Sokolich, or commuters. In response to media inquiries, Foye and the PA's spokesman would only say the closures were the subject of an "internal review," and did not estimate a time for completing the review.

Democrats in the New Jersey Assembly subpoenaed the emails and texts of those involved. Four months after the lane closures, in January 2014, more than a thousand pages of emails and text messages from before, during, and after the lane closures were released to the public.

On August 13, 2013, Bridget Anne Kelly, Deputy Chief of Staff for Governor Christie, emailed Deputy Executive Director David Wildstein.

Kelly: "Time for some traffic problems in Fort Lee."

Wildstein: "Got it."

Wildstein emailed Kelly on September 7.

Wildstein: "I will call you on Monday to let you know how Ft. Lee goes."

The next day, Wildstein directed PA employees to close two of the lanes leading onto the George Washington Bridge.

Ms. Kelly texted Wildstein on the morning of the second day of the lane closures.

Kelly: "I feel badly about the kids."

Wildstein: "They are the children of Buono voters."

State Senator Barbara Buono was Christie's Democratic opponent in the race for governor.

Fallout

The Christie administration initially said the lane closures were due to a poorly planned traffic study by Wildstein. At a press conference on December 2, 2013, Governor Christie's first public response to an inquiry on the lane closures was a flippant: "I worked the cones, actually. Unbeknownst to everybody I was actually the guy out there, in overalls and a hat." Addressing the reporter who asked about the lane closings, Christie chided, "You really are not serious with that question."

One month and one week after making these comments, Christie attempted to contain the scandal by holding a second press conference. At that time, he said, "[I am] responsible for what happens under my watch." He then denied any and all knowledge of the lane closures or involvement with its planning or execution. Christie also announced the firing of Ms. Kelly at the press conference.

The same day as this second press conference, Christie's appointee, Deputy Executive Director Baroni, was named as a defendant in a federal class action lawsuit that cited "willful, wanton, arbitrary, and egregious official misconduct." Wildstein resigned his $150,000 a year job from the PA four days after the press conference. Baroni resigned from the PA one week later. Both Wildstein and Baroni were subpoenaed to testify before the New Jersey General Assembly. Wildstein invoked his Fifth Amendment right against self-incrimination before the Assembly. Less than a month after their resignations, a federal grand jury opened an investigation into the lane closings.

Three years after the lane closures, in September 2016, a nine felony count trial for both Kelly and

Baroni began. Kelly is a single mother of four who has been unemployed since being fired by Christie.

Leaks Involving Potentially Illegal Activities

Sons and Daughters Program

Throughout the world, the ranks of CEOs and high-ranking government officials capable of influencing the placement of multimillion, and even multibillion dollar contracts are largely populated by men in their fifties and sixties. Many of these men have sons and daughters just graduating from college who are looking to launch their careers. This provides an opportunity for outside companies to offer a job to their children in an implicit agreement of receiving preferential consideration in the placement of a large contract.

The Wall Street Journal and *The New York Times* both ran multiple stories concerning J.P. Morgan's pursuit of contracts with Chinese industry and government agencies through a program called Referred Permanent Hires, informally known as the Sons and Daughters program, which was designed to hire children of Chinese officials and executives. The bank's

Human Resources, Compliance, and Legal departments oversaw the program. James "Jamie" Dimon, the CEO of J.P. Morgan, said in a January 2014 interview on CNBC that it had been the "norm of business for years" for banks to hire "sons and daughters of companies' [executives]" and to give them "proper jobs" without violating the law. "But we got to figure out exactly how to create a safe harbor for that so you don't...end up getting punished," he added.

The separate hiring track of the Sons and Daughters program gave heightened scrutiny to candidates to avoid the impression of improperly hiring children of highly placed parents just to win business. Over time, the process designed to prevent questionable hiring practices promoted them. Instead of being well qualified, some applicants from prominent Chinese families had subpar academic records and lacked relevant expertise.

The Wall Street Journal reviewed a document prepared by J.P. Morgan for submission to U.S. investigators in November 2015. The document listed 222 candidates hired by the bank under the Sons and Daughters program and the people who referred them. Nearly half the referrals came from government officials with the remainder from business executives and family members.

The program ran from 2004 to 2013. During that ten-year span, the bank worked on twelve Chinese initial public offerings (IPOs) of $1 billion or more, with the largest IPO being $22 billion. J.P. Morgan had previously hired sons or daughters of top executives at nine of the twelve IPOs. In 2010, 2011, and 2012, the peak hiring years of the program, the bank ranked third, fourteenth, and fourth in handling Chinese IPOs. After the bank closed the program, its Chinese IPO rankings dropped to twentieth in 2014 and twenty-fifth in 2015.

Bring Your Son to Their Work

William Daley, a senior executive with J.P. Morgan who was also a former U.S. Commerce Secretary and former White House Chief of Staff, met with Chinese Commerce Minister Gao Hucheng in July 2006. The meeting appeared to secure a job at J.P. Morgan for the minister's son, Gao Jue. Sherry Liu, a J.P. Morgan banker based in Hong Kong who helped set up the meeting, emailed Daley beforehand.

Liu: "a good in-depth relationship with the Ministry will pave the ground for us in many large and important industries in China…"

Within J.P. Morgan, Gao Jue was viewed as being uniquely unqualified, as outlined in an email by an internal J.P. Morgan recruiter, Danielle Domingue.

Domingue: "Jue did very very poorly in interviews — some MDs [managing directors] said he was the worst BA [business analyst] candidate they had ever see[n] — and we obviously had to extend him an offer…[because he] cam (*sic*) to us from Daley."

Jue was hired in July 2007 and was slated to be laid off amidst the financial crisis of 2008. However, his father intervened by having dinner with Fang Fang, Chief Executive Officer of China investment banking for J.P. Morgan. In an email after the dinner, Fang wrote a J.P. Morgan banker in New York.

Fang: "The father indicated to me repeatedly that he is willing to go extra miles to help JPM in whatever way we think he can. And I do have a few cases where I think we can leverage the father's connection."

Fang had received an email assessment of Jue's work performance earlier.

J.P. Morgan banker: "there is general consensus among the seniors in our group as well [as] reports from people in his previous group that he is immature, irresponsible and unreliable."

Jue was eventually given notice of termination in March 2009, and sequentially worked for what was then called Zurich Financial Services, the New York Stock Exchange, BNP Paribus in Hong Kong, Credit Suisse, and Goldman Sachs.

Don't Forget Your Daughter

J.P. Morgan pursued China's Tianhe Chemical Group (TCG) over a period of four years hoping to participate in the company's anticipated IPO. The daughter of the company's CEO, Joyce Wei, was hired by J.P. Morgan, but the bank backed away from working on the TCG IPO after U.S. regulators began investigating the bank for hiring the children of Chinese officials.

Emails showed that J.P. Morgan gave Ms. Wei a one-year contract, but she and her family sought a better deal, saying she had competing offers from other banks. J.P. Morgan raised her salary and Ms. Wei signed on. Only days after starting work in April 2011, more emails showed that she complained she was not getting a housing stipend or sign-on bonus like the other new hires and threatened to leave for a competitor. The bank again met her demands, stating in an internal email that her departure would "have material impact to our role and economics."

According to internal emails, J.P. Morgan initially thought it would be the sole underwriter for the IPO, but while negotiating Ms. Wei's benefits, they learned that TCG had hired three additional investment banks to run its IPO, significantly reducing J.P. Morgan's fees. One J.P. Morgan banker expressed his exasperation in an email.

Banker 1: "Beautiful — can we return the candidate to sender, maybe rotate amongst the 4 banks?"

Another banker wrote a sarcastic note regarding the lack of productivity seen in hires under the Sons and Daughters program.

Banker 2: "The associate we hired for you, Joyce Wei — can we make her do some real work or is she a protected species?"

Ms. Wei received mixed performance reviews, receiving praise for her language skills and positive attitude, but criticism for lack of attention to detail and lack of industry knowledge. Two years after joining the bank in July 2013, Ms. Wei was placed on a performance-improvement plan. Ms. Wei resigned from J.P. Morgan in August 2013. She left two weeks after J.P. Morgan disclosed that U.S. regulators were probing its hiring practices in Asia. UBS, a large international investment bank, was told informally by TCG around July 2013 that it would be hired to work on its IPO. Ms. Wei was hired by UBS three months later.

Is This Legal?

An SEC letter to J.P. Morgan in May 2013 outlined its request for "documents sufficient to identify all persons involved in the decision to hire." A year later, in its May 2014 SEC filings under the title of "Referral Hiring Practices Investigations," J.P. Morgan stated, "Various regulators are investigating, among other things, the Firm's compliance with the Foreign Corrupt Practices Act. The Firm is cooperating with these investigations."

There is nothing inherently illegal about hiring the children of well-connected people. The Foreign Corrupt Practices Act of 1977 does, however, bar U.S. companies from giving money or other items of value to foreign officials to win business, which would include a job to their children. To violate the law, a company must act with "corrupt" intent, or with the expectation of offering a job in exchange for government business.

How Did That Get Out?

An incompetent, spoiled adult child of a high-ranking executive receiving a job to secure future business is an interesting story, but the question that is never answered is how did *The Wall Street Journal* and *The New York Times* acquire multiple private emails from J.P. Morgan covering almost a decade?

The Wall Street Journal used phrases such as "according to documents prepared for a presentation that were reviewed by the *Journal*," and "according to separate documents reviewed by the *Journal*," but never tells the reader the source of these documents. With the SEC investigation starting in May 2013 and the first story appearing in *The New York Times* in August 2013, it seems to indicate the supporting emails were leaked from someone inside the SEC or J.P. Morgan to *The New York Times*. An email sent by this writer to *The New York Times* seeking clarification was not answered.

Leaks Designed to Make the Sender Look Incompetent or Disingenuous

"…Crash the Plane at Takeoff."

The Affordable Care Act (ACA), referred to as Obamacare, was the cornerstone of President Obama's domestic policy. It was designed to address rapidly rising health care costs and offer coverage for approximately forty million uninsured Americans. Taking the website HealthCare.gov live was intended to kick-start the program by allowing millions of

Americans to register for health care benefits. The design of the website was overseen by the Centers for Medicare and Medicaid Services (CMS) and built by the CGI Group of Canada.

The HealthCare.gov website was launched as planned on October 1, 2013 and immediately revealed serious problems. Stress tests performed by contractors the day before the launch found the site was so slow it was almost unusable with only 1,100 simulated simultaneous users. When opened, the site drew 250,000 actual simultaneous users, but only 1 percent of them were able to enroll in the first week. Website visitors were required to create an account before being able to compare health care plans and the registration process created a bottleneck leading to what CNN called "maddeningly long wait times." Insurance providers reported applications missing required information, probably because pull-down menus worked only sporadically.

Challenges with the website mirrored internal conflicts between the contractors and the federal government. CGI missed various deadlines before the October 1 launch date. On July 8, a federal official had written an email expressing his concerns about CGI.

Federal official: "…they have never revealed the seriously substandard level of staffing that this team has…We believe that our entire build is in jeopardy."

CGI's employees claimed the problem was not the company's work, but a lack of direction as the CMS argued over what tasks should take priority. "This is internal infighting and reflects the lack of a strong, single manager at CMS to drive the program," one CGI employee said.

Henry Chao, Deputy Chief Information Officer at the CMS, emailed more than two dozen federal officials telling them CGI needed to accelerate the pace of work.

Chao: "I just need to feel more confident they are not going to crash the plane at takeoff."

Another email from Chao stated that he and his boss, Marilyn Tavenner, the Administrator of CMS, testified before Congress earlier that month.

Chao: "Marilyn and I under oath stated that we are going to make October 1."

Days before the planned October 1 launch, Chao emailed dozens of his colleagues.

Chao: "I DO NOT WANT A REPEAT OF WHAT HAPPENED NEAR THE END OF DECEMBER 2005, WHERE MEDICARE.GOV HAD A MELTDOWN."

His concerns were not allayed when he received an email two days before launch from Akhtar Zaman, a Health and Human Services computer systems integrator.

Zaman: "We'll be continue (*sic*) to test today, tomorrow and beyond until we reach at least 10k concurrent users, and eventually 50K."

Fallout

Before the website launch, Obama said it was "on track" and was upbeat in his public comments. A month after the botched website launch, Republican Fred Upton, Chairman of the House Energy and Commerce Committee, released eleven pages of emails that contradicted the previous, optimistic outlook Obama gave Congress concerning the website.

"The Administration went out of its way to hide the chaos behind the scenes," Representative Upton said. Upton did not mention how he acquired private emails sent using official government email accounts. At a news conference in November 2013, President Obama said that had he been "informed directly that the website would not be working the way it was supposed to...I wouldn't be going out saying, 'Boy, this is going to be great!'"

...and how to avoid them

If you don't know the answer to a question, don't guess, don't speculate, don't hypothesize, and don't make a joke about it by email, tweet, conference call, or at a press conference. When the Executive Director of the Port Authority was asked about the lane closures, he simply responded that it was under "internal review." Somehow, eventually, the electronic communication surrounding a situation will be made public and clarify what actually transpired. Governor Christie did not help his image by sarcastically answering that he moved the traffic cones himself when asked about the lane closures.

In comments made electronically, on conference calls, or in press conferences, be diplomatic. The assessment by J.P. Morgan bankers of Gao Jue as "immature, irresponsible, and unreliable" would have been better written as "does not meet the bank's hiring standards." The snide emails asking if Joyce Wei was a "protected species" and "can we return candidate to sender" should not have been written. The only purpose they now serve is to validate the SEC's claim of giving jobs in exchange for contracts.

Politics has been called as war by other means, with words being the other means. In the Darwinian environment of business, one's most provocative words are naturally selected by competitors to be hurled back at the writer at the most inopportune moment. Do not arm your adversaries.

Per Our Agreement

If You Love Something, Never Let It Go

Oil companies are valued on proven oil reserves. Car companies are measured by the number of cars sold annually. Tech companies realized early on that people truly are their most valuable asset. In 1986, George Lucas sold the computer-generated animation division of Lucasfilm to Steve Jobs, who renamed the division Pixar. Lucas believed that Lucasfilm, and the newly independent Pixar, should not compete against each other for employees because "it was not a normal industrial competitive situation" and they didn't "have the margins for that sort of thing." This sentiment was echoed by Pixar President Edward Catmull, who claimed bidding for employees "messes up the pay structure." To help hold down operating costs, Lucasfilm and Pixar agreed: (1) not to cold-call each other's employees to offer them jobs, (2) to notify each other when making an offer to an employee of the other company, and (3) that any job offer would be final. Although beneficial to Lucasfilm and Pixar, this anticompetitive arrangement was a violation of the Sherman Antitrust Act.

Steve Jobs soon expanded the Pixar-Lucasfilm agreement to include Apple. Pixar needed to obtain Jobs's permission before making an offer to any Apple employee. Pixar Vice President of Human Resources Lori McAdams told her recruiting team, "Effective now, we'll follow a gentleman's agreement with Apple that is similar to our Lucasfilm agreement. That is...we won't directly solicit any Apple employee."

The CEOs of tech giants often sat on one another's boards, acted as consultants for one another's companies, and met socially. The entire web of "gentlemen's agreements" expanded to include some of the biggest tech companies and was enforced, clarified, and documented by emails.

Never Mind

In 2005, Jobs complained to Bruce Chizen, the CEO of Adobe, about Adobe recruiting Apple employees. Chizen responded in an email that he thought their agreement only applied to senior level executives.

Chizen: "I thought we agreed not to recruit any senior level employees...I would propose we keep it that way. Open to discuss. It would be good to agree."

Jobs was not satisfied and threatened to have Apple start recruiting Adobe employees.

Jobs: "OK, I'll tell our recruiters that they are free to approach any Adobe employee who is not a Sr. Director or VP. Am I understanding your position correctly?"

Chizen immediately emailed back.

Chizen: "I'd rather agree NOT to actively solicit any employee from either company...If you are in agreement I will let my folks know."

The next day, Theresa Townsley, Adobe Vice President of Human Resources, announced to her recruiting team, "Bruce and Steve Jobs have an agreement that we are not to solicit ANY Apple employees, and vice versa."

The Email Trail

In 2005, Apple and Google agreed not to recruit each other's employees. A recruiter working on behalf of Google violated the agreement, and Jobs complained to Eric Schmidt, Google Executive Chairman, in an email. Schmidt replied to Jobs by email.

Schmidt: "Steve, as a followup (sic) we investigated the recruiter's actions and she violated our policies."

Schmidt then attached an internal email from Google recruiting to Jobs.

Google recruiting: "On this specific case, the sourcer [external recruiter] who contacted this Apple employee should not have and will be terminated within the hour. In general, we have a very clear 'do not call' policy (attached) that is given to every staffing professional and I reiterate the message in ongoing communications and staff meetings."

Jobs was pleased by Schmidt's quick response to his complaint.

Jobs: ":) Steve"

After the Google-Apple agreement was in place, Google instituted its own no-poaching agreements with numerous firms. To keep track of which companies had an agreement with Google, its HR department was asked to compile a Do Not Call list, which Schmidt approved.

Schmidt: "this looks very good."

When Shona Brown, a Google executive, emailed Schmidt asking if he had any concerns about sharing the Do Not Call list with Google's competitors, Schmidt replied by email that he preferred it be shared verbally.

Schmidt: "verbally[,] since I don't want to create a paper trail over which we can be sued later?"

Shona Brown replied by email.

Brown: "makes sense to do orally. i agree."

Their email exchange created the paper trail he wanted to avoid.

Intel was one of the companies on Google's list. In an email to an Intel recruiter in April 2007, Paul Otellini, the CEO of Intel as well as a member of the Google board of directors, explained their non-compete agreement with Google.

Otellini: "I have an unofficial no-poaching policy with Google."

Schmidt confirmed the policy in a June 2007 email to Otellini.

Schmidt: "I checked as to our recruiting policy with Intel. Intel has been listed on the Do Not Call List since the policy was created. No one in staffing directly calls, networks, or emails into the company or its subsidiaries looking for talent. Hopefully there are no exceptions to this policy and if you become aware of this please let me know immediately!"

An Intel recruiter asked Otellini and another senior executive about the existence of a no-poaching policy in another email exchange.

Intel recruiter: "Are either of you aware of any agreement with Google that prohibits us from recruiting Google's senior talent?"

Otellini: "Let me clarify. We have nothing signed. We have a handshake 'no recruit' between eric and myself. I would not like this broadly known."

Standing Up to the Bully

Steve Jobs attempted to arrange a no-poaching agreement with Palm Technology after several employees moved between the two companies. According to court filings, in August 2007, Jobs called Ed Colligan, President and CEO of Palm, to propose "an arrangement between Palm and Apple by which neither company would hire the other's employees, including high tech employees."

Colligan related that Jobs threatened to retaliate against Palm if he did not join the agreement. "Mr. Jobs also suggested that if Palm did not agree to such an arrangement, Palm could face lawsuits alleging infringement of Apple's many patents." Colligan wrote Jobs an email refusing to acquiesce to Jobs's demands.

Colligan: "your proposal that we agree that neither company will hire the other's employees, regardless of the individual's desires, is not only wrong, it is likely illegal. I can't deny people who elect to pursue their livelihood at Palm the right to do so simply because they now work for Apple, and I wouldn't want you to do that to current Palm employees...I want to be clear that we are not intimidated by your threat...If you choose the litigation route, we can respond with our claims based on [Palm's] patent assets, but I don't think litigation is the answer."

Jobs: "This is not satisfactory to Apple...We must do whatever we can to stop this. I'm sure you realize the asymmetry in the financial resources of our respective companies when you say: "We will both

just end up paying a lot of lawyers a lot of money."…
My advice is to take a look at our patent portfolio
before you make a final decision here."

Colligan did not communicate with Jobs further
regarding the proposal.

Follow the Money

Complicating the need for a highly trained work
force, Silicon Valley employers had another serious
problem. Droves of people were making millions of
dollars very, very quickly. Of the $48 billion of venture
capital invested in the United States in 2014, over
half was invested in firms located in Silicon Valley.
Software and Internet-based companies received
$31.7 billion in venture capital, the largest invest-
ment since the height of the dotcom boom in 2000.
"The returns on investment are just too healthy to
ignore for people who want to put cash into the market," said Mark McCaffrey, software industry expert.

The company WhatsApp, founded in 2009,
was an example of returns "too healthy to ignore."
WhatsApp charged users ninety-nine cents per
year to send pictures, texts, and videos using their

cellphones. Unlike most Internet and mobile messaging startups, it did not accept ads, which helps explain its net loss of $138 million in 2014. However, the loss did not dissuade Facebook from buying WhatsApp in 2014 for just under $22 billion.

The problem for existing tech companies was how to prevent their highly trained employees from leaving for startups or the rapidly expanding Facebook. Sergey Brin, a Google cofounder, addressed the challenge of employees leaving Google in an email to other company executives in October 2007.

Brin: "The Facebook phenomenon creates a real retention problem, I now realize, not just because of FB's direct hiring, but the more insidious effect that everyone wants to start the next Facebook or get rich by having a popular fb app."

In August 2008, Bill Campbell, Chairman of the Intuit Board of Directors, Co-Lead Director of Apple, and advisor to Google, addressed the issue of Facebook raiding talent from other tech companies in an email to Google executives.

Campbell: "Who should contact Sheryl [Sandberg, Facebook COO] or Mark [Zuckerberg, Facebook CEO] to get a cease-fire? We have to get a truce."

Incredibly, Sandberg had been a Google Vice-President only five months earlier and was now being asked to stop recruiting her former Google colleagues. Sandberg said in a court deposition, "I declined at that time to limit Facebook's recruitment or hiring of Google employees."

Google closely tracked the percentage of its technical candidates who rejected job offers, presumably because they received a better offer elsewhere in Silicon Valley. During 2010, Facebook accounted for the highest proportion of overall departures. Brin started receiving regular reports of how many Google employees left for Facebook and how many Facebook employees joined Google. Schmidt, Google Executive Chairman, later described the situation, "[in 2008] Facebook's management structure was being built of executives coming out of Google."

In June 2008, Google executive Shona Brown emailed colleagues.

Brown: "really doubling down our efforts to recruit back [from Facebook]…to stem the tide and give us better negotiating position on a recruiting truce."

Having seen many of its fellow employees leave for the potential of stock riches at Facebook, Google surveyed its people to learn what would induce them to stay. The survey revealed the answer was simply higher salaries.

Ironically, Google was the hot tech company accused of increasing salaries only three years earlier in 2005. At that time, Meg Whitman, former CEO of eBay, told Schmidt directly, "Google is the talk of the Valley because [Google is] driving up salaries across the board."

Tangled Web

After twenty-three years, the DOJ somehow found out about the "gentlemen's agreements" and opened an investigation in 2009. At that time, the no-poaching agreement had grown to include Adobe, Apple, Google, Intel, Intuit, Lucasfilm, and Pixar, all of which settled a DOJ lawsuit in 2011 for conspiring not to recruit one another's employees.

The DOJ suit did not include monetary damages for the employees who had been aggrieved, so a second lawsuit was brought against the same companies seeking damages of $3 billion on behalf of 64,000 current and former employees potentially harmed by the arrangement. Both lawsuits were largely built on emails written by the defendants. In March 2015, Adobe, Apple, Google, Intel, Lucasfilm, and Pixar agreed to a settlement of $415 million for the second lawsuit. Intuit settled separately.

...and how to avoid them

Most people could not cite the Sherman Antitrust Act of 1890 as the basis for why these agreements were illegal, but most people innately recognize they were unethical. Although the tech companies benefited from the agreements, they were legally and morally wrong. None of the CEOs had a contract drawn up by their Legal department because they knew they were wrong.

At the time Jobs threatened to cripple Palm through patent lawsuits, Apple was approximately one hundred times larger than Palm and 100 percent capable of fulfilling the threat. Much to his credit, the CEO of Palm did not let the power disparity alter his moral compass. Colligan documented their phone call by emailing Jobs an emphatic refusal to participate. Jobs unwisely documented his verbal threats in an email reply to Colligan. One leader used email to his advantage and one used email to his detriment.

The settlement of $415 million was equal to slightly over one half of one day's earnings for Apple, Adobe, Intel, and Google collectively, leading some to argue that the no-poaching agreement made good sense financially. However, after settling two lawsuits, the employees of those companies know that at the highest levels, maximizing corporate earnings by minimizing employees' earnings was a long-term corporate strategy that was aggressively pursued. As summarized by Google cofounder Sergey Brin, "[Jobs] said 'if you hire a single one of these people [Apple employees] that means war." The strategy of treating people as a commodity stripped them of their inherent humanity and undermined the loyalty and commitment of those people the CEOs fought so ferociously to retain.

BREATHE. THINK. REPLY.

The Primacy of Information

Since the advent of the personal computer, it has been said we live in the Information Age. However, the success of an individual or a society has always depended upon the timely application of relevant information — where to find buffalo, how to grow rice, or what fruit should not be eaten. Military victories are often attributed to superior information. A company's proprietary information, as measured by its patent portfolio, correlates directly with its success.

Information Generates Wealth

The internal combustion engine has a four-stroke cycle: Intake — air-fuel mixture is drawn in;

Compression — air-fuel mixture is pressed into close contact; Power — sparkplug firing forces piston down; and Exhaust — spent gases are expelled. Wealth propagation in Washington D.C. is a three-stroke cycle: Intake — money buys access; Compression — access provides information; and Power — information generates more money. Corporations, labor unions, and political action committees spent $3.2 billion in 2015 on the services of 11,515 registered lobbyists. Of those, the largest group is the health lobby, consisting of health care insurers, HMOs, pharmaceutical companies, hospitals, and health care professionals.

Traditionally, the role of a lobbyist has been to influence lawmakers for the benefit of their clients. However, in the relatively new industry of political intelligence, lobbyists may be used to gain information rather than to exert influence. Lobbyists and others in the political intelligence industry collect information from elected officials, the aides of elected officials, regulators, and anyone else who might offer insight into proposed laws and regulatory changes. Access is often gained by making campaign contributions or through the contacts the lobbyist made on Capitol Hill when working in the federal government.

In early 2013, the Centers for Medicare and Medicaid Services (CMS) proposed cutting the Medicare Advantage program, a decision that would cost health care insurance companies collectively about $8 billion per year. Two groups had a large financial interest in the proposed cuts: health care insurers and large, institutional investors that invested in health care insurers. Lobbyists for health care insurers tried to persuade lawmakers to reverse the proposed cuts while political intelligence operatives working for investors sought information on a potential reversal *before* such information became public. It was possible for one lobbyist to be working for a health care insurer as a lobbyist while simultaneously gathering political intelligence for large investors. With billions in revenue and stock market valuation at stake, any information about the possibility of a reversal by the CMS was at a premium.

The Quest for Information

Height Securities is a political intelligence firm that gathers information on government regulations, court rulings, tax and budget changes, and other issues that may impact industry sectors or the move-ments of the stock market as a whole. Its website contains the statements, "Research is the engine that drives all facets of our business," and "We have a passion for policy and the markets."

If Height Securities provided its clients with credible information of a reversal, health care stocks could be bought, and hopefully sold, at a profit, after the CMS publicly announced a reversal. Information obtained by Height Securities and disseminated to its clients, although not confidential, was not readily available to the public.

Justin Simon, a health care analyst with Height Securities, sought information on the proposed CMS funding cuts to pass along to his clients of hedge funds and institutional investors. Since the announcement by the CMS of the proposed fund-ing cuts, Simon had been exchanging emails with his Washington contacts, pressing for information. One of his contacts was Stephanie Carlton, a health care aide for the senior Republican on the Finance Committee, Senator Orrin Hatch (R, UT). Another of Simon's contacts was Mark Hayes, a former senior health care aide for Senator Charles Grassley (R, IA).

A Picture of Information Generating Wealth

Consulting firms routinely arrange private conference calls between public officials and their institutional clients of pension funds, mutual funds, and hedge funds. The possibility of health care insurance companies recovering $8 billion dollars in revenue from the federal government was so large that numerous entities were attempting to discern what the ultimate CMS decision would be. One such firm, Capitol Street, arranged a call with staffers in Senator Hatch's office on March 18, 2013 to discuss the possibility of the CMS reversing its proposed budget cuts.

An analyst at Capitol Street recorded the conference call and *The Washington Post* printed excerpts from it in May 2013. On the conference call, Stephanie Carlton was pressed by the Capitol Hill consultant to predict if the CMS would restore the funding cuts for Medicare Advantage. Carlton said, "…if I were assigning probabilities 0 to 100 percent, I would have said 5 to 10 percent likelihood…a month ago. I would move it up to maybe 30, 35 percent probability that they change it." She said she was "definitely more optimistic," and if they were ever going to change the Medicare policy, "this would be the year to do it."

Humana is a health care insurer that writes Medicare Advantage plans and would have benefited from a reversal of the planned CMS cuts. Immediately after the conference call ended, at 11:05 a.m., the volume of call options in Humana spiked nearly ten times as much as any day in the previous two weeks. Call options are a financial instrument bought when anticipating a rise in a stock price. Presumably, the options were purchased by investors who were on the conference call.

Who Do You Work For?

Greenberg Traurig is one of the nation's largest law and lobbying firms, and it was also engaged in political intelligence gathering for a time. Two years before the Capitol Street conference call with Senator Hatch's office, Height Securities, the firm that employed Justin Simon, retained Greenberg Traurig to provide Height with information that could potentially impact health care legislation. Mark Hayes was Simon's contact at Greenberg Traurig.

Hayes began his career as a registered pharmacist and later worked for different Republican senators as an aide specializing in health care law. In the mid-1990s, he helped draft the Republican response to the Clinton health care plan. While working as an aide, Hayes served as the Health Policy Director of the Senate Finance Committee and helped craft the Medicare prescription drug benefit bill. *Roll Call*, the Capitol Hill newspaper, wrote that a former aide dubbed him "The 101st Senator" due to his influence. Chris Jennings, a Democratic health care consultant, called Hayes "smart, respected, and liked." In 2010, the forty-six-year-old Hayes leveraged his twenty years of political experience by joining Greenberg Traurig as both a health care lobbyist as well as a political intelligence operative in the health care industry.

Lobbyists are registered and publicly disclosed. However, there is no public disclosure of who may be working in political intelligence. Additionally, there is no regulation preventing a lobbyist from simultaneously gathering political intelligence, so public officials do not know if a lobbyist is also passing along tidbits of information from their conversations to large, professional stock traders.

One Email, One Reply, Four Federal Investigations

At 3:09 p.m. on April 1, 2013, Simon emailed Hayes asking about rumors that the CMS would reverse the proposed budget cuts. A few minutes later, Hayes replied he had learned from "very credible sources" that the CMS had decided to reverse its decision: "Our intel is the deal was already hatched." Hayes further explained the reversal was in exchange for Senator Hatch's support of an Obama nominee. Simon attempted to confirm the deal by forwarding Hayes's email to contacts in Washington, including an aide to Senator Hatch and a lobbyist for Humana. He did not receive a reply from either.

Thirty-three minutes after receiving the initial email from Hayes, and eighteen minutes before the markets closed, Simon sent an email to over one hundred of Height Securities' clients. The volume of stock trading in Humana, United Health, Aetna, and other health insurance companies spiked in the remaining minutes of trading. That same day, after the markets closed, the CMS announced that the proposed funding cuts for Medicare Advantage would not be implemented. The following morning, Humana, United Health, and Aetna opened up by 6 to 7 percent. Investors who purchased call options after the conference call held with Senator Hatch's office on March 18, and who sold after the public announcement of the CMS decision on April 1, made an astounding five-fold return in less than two weeks.

The next morning, when Hayes learned that information from his email had been forwarded, he fired off an angry email to Simon.

Hayes: "Very bad. I have a lot of damage control to do on multiple fronts because of this."

Simon: "There is nothing I can say to describe the level of embarrassment and remorse I feel over the situation. I will not be able to sleep over it tonight."

After *The Wall Street Journal* reported the chain of events on April 17, 2013, the SEC, CMS, and FBI began separate investigations. Hayes's former boss, Senator Grassley, also initiated an investigation into Hayes' activities. The senator said of his friend and former aide, "I valued Mark Hayes greatly on my committee staff, and I know him to be a good person." Senator Grassley's staff interviewed Hayes twice. Simon was subpoenaed to testify about the email he received from Hayes and to list the clients he emailed.

Hayes was fired by one of his clients and took a leave of absence from Greenberg Traurig after the article appeared in *The Wall Street Journal*. The SEC interviewed Hayes with the FBI present for four hours. The SEC and the Justice Department sent subpoenas to the House Ways and Means Committee and to their top aides seeking documents and testimony to ascertain if Congressional staffers tipped Hayes to the pending change in health care policy. These were the first formal requests for information involving a Congressional insider-trading investigation in almost a decade.

Insider Tip or Mosaic Theory?

The crux of the issue was whether Hayes obtained his tip from government officials, which could violate the STOCK Act, or whether his email reflected his own analysis, which is legal. The STOCK Act of 2012, an acronym for Stop Trading on Congressional Knowledge, tightened insider-trading rules for lawmakers and their aides. The law prohibits public officials, aides, or bureaucrats from disclosing any nonpublic information that could affect stock prices, but does not prohibit aides and elected officials from speaking with lobbyists, investors, and consultants. Lobbyists with close ties to former colleagues on Capitol Hill may offer their analysis from multiple conversations. Basing predictions on multiple small data points, none clearly indicative by themselves, is a permissible practice and referred to in the political intelligence industry as the Mosaic Theory.

Hayes told Senator Grassley's investigators that his prediction was based on his own analysis, not a specific tip. He said one of the facts that formed his opinion came from Senator Grassley's current health care aide, Rodney Whitlock. When Hayes left to become a lobbyist, Whitlock, his subordinate, became the senior health care aide. Being involved in health care policy, both men remained in close contact through email and lunches. The spokeswoman for Senator Grassley said that during a meeting in March, and in subsequent emails, Whitlock relayed information to Hayes that the Senate was planning a confirmation hearing for the interim head of the CMS. A spokeswoman for Senator Grassley's office said, "Rodney and Mark have talked regularly, as might be expected, given their positions." In May 2013, the Justice Department hand-delivered a letter to Senator Grassley's office, asking for the emails between Whitlock and Hayes.

…and how to avoid them

Every employee, at every level, is governed by numerous regulations and corporate policies. Mark Hayes, an attorney and lobbyist with twenty years of experience on Capitol Hill, had to be aware of the recently enacted laws written specifically for federal lawmakers concerning trading on insider information. Justin Simon, employed to gather tips that could be profitably traded, had to be aware of the same laws. But both, feeling the pressure of time, put information into emails and passed that information on to others. Within hours, that information proved to be explosive.

In response to Simon's request for information, if Hayes had written a short reply like, "My analysis indicates the CMS will probably reverse the proposed funding cuts," he would have protected himself under Mosaic Theory, sparing himself multiple investigations and a leave of absence from his job. Be brief and choose your words judiciously in answering emails.

The eight billion dollars in revenue at stake in the Medicare funding decision is an excellent example that the more valuable the information in an email, the greater the likelihood it will be forwarded. Forwarding an email containing sensitive information to people outside your company is almost always a poor decision.

Business is an ongoing, never-ending series of deadlines. The pressure to meet a deadline can cause the sender not to evaluate critically what has been written in an email. A sense of urgency should act as a warning, a yellow caution light, to slow down and look both ways before proceeding. The extra couple of minutes may pay massive dividends in avoiding problems that can arise almost immediately.

You Have the Right to Remain Silent

Face Time

One hundred and six people, including eighty retired police officers and firefighters, were indicted by a grand jury for disability fraud in January 2014. The defendants had received more than $21 million in benefits. Many claimed they could no longer work or lead active lives, yet investigators found pictures and videos posted on Facebook, Twitter, and YouTube of them playing basketball, riding jet skis, and flying helicopters. One man who had claimed to be virtually housebound was photographed holding a marlin he caught while in Costa Rica.

Newspapers once featured pictures of criminals being led out of courthouses covering their faces with their hands. Some speculated that they enjoyed the smell of their hands; perhaps so, but a more plausible explanation is that they did not want a picture of their face associated with their actions. Poor judgment cannot be eradicated, but the propensity to document one's lack of discretion to one's detriment might be attenuated with a few examples.

"My Day Is Empty and Without Purpose"

Dennis Lerner, a 60-year-old IRS tax examiner, conducted an audit of Commerzbank and discovered $1 billion in unreported income. This led to Commerzbank paying the IRS an additional $210 million in taxes in 2013. While conducting the audit, Lerner interviewed for the position of Tax Director at Commerzbank without notifying his IRS supervisor, a violation of conflict of interest laws. Pending the settlement of the audit, he resigned from the IRS and started working for Commerzbank.

During the subsequent criminal investigation of Lerner's conduct, his personal emails were examined. Those emails showed he repeatedly complained about his IRS job. In one email, he wrote "I need to see my idiot manager," and continued with, "I get paid next to nothing and work with fools." "My day is empty and without purpose."

Lerner received a $10,000 fine and 150 hours of community service. He could have been sentenced to ten months in prison. When he appeared in the Manhattan federal court, Lerner apologized and told U.S. District Judge John Keenan he "used very poor judgment." The judge responded, "You certainly did," and called Lerner's decisions "dopey."

Warning: Tweeting May Prove Hazardous to Your Career

Jofi Joseph led a double life. He was the White House Director of Nuclear Nonproliferation on the National Security Council, whose oversight included both North Korea and Iran. He also anonymously wrote the Twitter account @NatSecWonk, which, within Washington D.C., was widely popular. In one NatSecWonk post, "Unapologetically says what everyone else only thinks" on "the foreign policy and national security scene." "I'm abrasive and I bring the snark." Over the course of two years, NatSecWonk's tweets berated and insulted public figures, reporters, and even his own colleagues. His tweets did not disclose any national security secrets, but were more sophomoric and spiteful in nature.

Joseph tweeted his opinion of Hillary Clinton when she was Secretary of State.

Joseph: "[Clinton] had few policy goals and no wins."

He tweeted his opinion of Vice President Joe Biden as well.

Joseph: "Interesting factoid: Both Tom Donilon and Tony Blinken once worked for Biden. Both of their wives work for the VP today. #incestuous."

Joseph repeatedly accused Deputy National Security Advisor for Strategic Communications Ben Rhodes of dodging questions about Benghazi.

Joseph: "Look, [Republican representative Darrell] Issa is an ass, but he's on to something here with the @HillaryClinton whitewash of accountability for Benghazi."

The White House and State Department had been searching for the accountholder of NatSecWonk. This search intensified after Joseph's numerous tweets questioned the validity of the official version of the September 11, 2012 attacks on the Benghazi embassy, which left four Americans dead, including U.S. Ambassador to Libya Christopher Stephens. The investigation looked at locations from where NatSecWonk tweets originated and matched them to Joseph's travel, thereby identifying him as the author. In October 2013, lawyers from the White House counsel's office confronted Joseph at work about his tweets and escorted him from the executive complex. Joseph had been scheduled to rotate out of his White House duties to a senior job in the Pentagon.

Joseph was a familiar figure in foreign policy circles. The revelation that he was NatSecWonk came as a shock because he was generally well respected and popular. His wife, Carolyn Leddy, is a highly regarded staffer on the Republican side of the Senate Foreign Relations Committee.

Joseph took down his NatSecWonk account and apologized for his tweets in remarks to Politico, an online political commentary website. "What started out as an intended parody account of D.C. culture developed over time into a series of inappropriate and mean-spirited comments. I bear complete responsibility for this affair and I sincerely apologize to everyone I insulted. It has been a privilege to serve in this Administration and I deeply regret violating the trust and confidence placed in me."

Tweets Don't Delay Senate Confirmations, People Do

In November 2013, President Obama nominated Dr. Vivek Murthy to become the U.S. Surgeon General. Dr. Murthy received his bachelor's degree from Harvard and his medical degree from Yale. Most surgeon generals are chosen from physicians who have run a countrywide health care system or were the chief medical officer of a hospital. At age thirty-five, Murthy had only been a licensed physician for eight years and had never been the head of a hospital department.

Dr. Murthy's credentials did include founding "Doctors for Obama" to help elect President Obama in 2008. After the president's election, Murthy renamed the organization "Doctors for America." The organization supported expanding the federal government's role in health care and what eventually became the Affordable Care Act, or Obamacare.

Murthy's support of Obamacare and lack of experience were not what proved problematic in his confirmation hearings. What raised the hackles of the NRA and almost cost him his senate confirmation was one twenty-word, 98-character tweet he had sent a year earlier.

Murthy: "Tired of politicians playing politics [with] guns, putting lives at risk [because] they're scared of NRA. Guns are a health care issue."

Concerned that Murthy would use his position as surgeon general as a platform to push gun control as a public health issue, the NRA sent a letter to U.S. senators in March 2014, informing them that the NRA opposed his nomination. Chris Cox, Executive Director of the NRA's Institute for Legislative Action, appeared on Fox News to make the case against Murthy. Cox stated the NRA would factor each senator's vote on Murthy into the grade the NRA would assign that senator before their next election.

Five days after the NRA was on Fox News, the White House press secretary was asked if the Obama administration planned to abandon Murthy's nomination. The secretary replied, "We expect him to get confirmed ultimately and be one of the country's most powerful messengers on health and wellness," adding, "We're recalibrating our approach, but in answer to your question, no." After more than a year of delay, the Senate confirmed Murthy for surgeon general in December 2014. The vote was 53-41, split along party lines, with one Republican breaking rank to support the nomination.

Pride Goeth Before the Fall

In the summer of 2012, people across the nation were protesting comments made by a Chick-fil-A executive against same-sex marriage. Thirty-four-year-old Adam Smith was the CFO of Vante, a Tucson-based medical device manufacturer, with a salary of $200,000 a year and stock options valued at over a million dollars. Smith wanted to support the ongoing protests and went to a Chick-fil-A drive-thru to ask for a glass of water. While there, he used his cellphone to film a tirade against Chick-fil-A that was directed toward the young female employee giving him the free glass of water.

Smith: "Chick-fil-A is a hateful corporation. I don't know how you live with yourself and work here. I don't understand it."

Smith posted his video on YouTube before returning to work. Arriving back at his office, the receptionist told him "the voicemail is completely full, and it's full of bomb threats." Smith was fired that day, losing his $200,000 a year salary and stock options. He moved with his wife and four children to Portland where he worked as a CFO for another company for two weeks before his employer learned about the YouTube posting and fired him. Smith said he has been upfront about the posting in interviews since the Portland job, but companies do not want to risk that it will happen again. As of 2015, Smith was living with his wife and children in an RV and using food stamps to feed his family.

...and how to avoid them

For every opinion, there is an equal and opposite opinion. Every topic upon which you comment on social media is open for viewing by employers, clients, and competitors. In today's business environment, presume that some of your followers may intend to exploit your opinions to their advantage and your detriment. Facts are more difficult to refute, so post a fact instead of an opinion. Had Murthy tweeted, "According to the CDC, in 2013, 33,804 Americans died from wounds inflicted by guns," it would have been more difficult for the NRA to attack him.

"You have the right to remain silent. Anything you say, can and will be used against you in a court of law...Do you understand the rights I have just read to you? With these rights in mind, do you wish to speak to me?" Most American adults have heard the Miranda rights from countless television and movie crime dramas. The first statement of the Miranda rights is a simple but powerful declarative sentence. "You have the right to remain silent." Not speaking will not be held against you, but the suspect is told that any words spoken "can and will be used against you in a court of law." U.S. law provides the *opportunity* for reflection and protection against self-incrimination with the last sentence asking, "Do you wish to speak to me?" Reflect and ask yourself, is it wise to post or send an email containing that information?

The First Amendment protects a broad freedom of expression. However, there is no legal protection from the consequences of those expressions. Title VII of the Civil Rights Act of 1964 protects applicants and employees from discrimination in hiring, firing, promotion, and other aspects of employment on the basis of race, religion, gender, or national origin. There is no protection for employees or applicants for public expression of opinions on controversial subjects. According to a 2013 survey by CareerBuilder, 39 percent of employers had conducted a search of candidates on social media sites and 43 percent had eliminated a candidate from consideration for a job due to information or photos found.

The Director of Nuclear Nonproliferation, the U.S. Surgeon General, and the CFO did not commit any crimes, but the words they posted in minutes destroyed two careers and delayed a third. Whether at work in front of a computer or standing in line waiting for a cup of coffee using a cellphone, appreciate the life-altering power of words. Do not confuse the familiar for the benign.

CHEATING IN CONGRESS

Remember Who Owns It

Companies often provide their employees with computers, networks, and cellphones for the performance of their duties. Most companies have a written policy governing the use of their equipment that is rarely read because it is densely worded legal jargon. However, the main points are critical.

The standard policy states that the corporation owns, and therefore has access to, anything an employee reads, writes, posts, tweets, or texts using the corporation's equipment. There is no right to privacy regarding any information maintained on company property or transmitted through the company's computer network, voicemail, email, or Internet, including private email and social media accounts that are password protected. All are subject to search, monitoring, and review at the company's discretion without notice. To protect the company's legitimate business interests, the company may require an employee to provide their password(s) in order to facilitate monitoring of the employee's accounts. Personal use of any of the company's equipment and systems is a privilege that may be revoked at any time.

Forward

Emails forwarded to media outlets embarrass organizations and may lead to external investigations. Most organizations possess the technical capabilities to track down who forwarded an internal email to an outside email account. The natural inclination is to use these tracking abilities to censor or dismiss the leakers. A case study in how not to investigate email leaks was provided by a Harvard cheating scandal.

Define "Inappropriate Collaboration"

In August 2012, Harvard disclosed that almost half of the 279 students in Government 1310: Introduction to Congress were suspected of plagiarism and "inappropriate collaboration" on the take-home final exam from the previous May. Harvard called the cheating scandal "unprecedented in scope and magnitude." According to Harvard's internal rating of classes, Introduction to Congress was rated as "Easy" to "Very Easy." Class attendance was optional and the professor encouraged collaboration. There were four take-home exams, including the final exam, which students were given one week to complete. The professor instructed the class that the final exam was "open book, open note, and open Internet," but collaboration with fellow students was prohibited. An investigation was triggered when a teaching fellow grading the short-answer test noticed identical answers, including typographcal errors.

The administrative board investigates all allegations of cheating at Harvard and metes out punishment as it deems warranted. Jay Ellison was secretary of the board. Other members of the board included Harvard's sixteen resident deans and Evelynn Hammonds, dean of Harvard College.

In the course of their investigation, the administrative board learned that although Introduction to Congress had been previously rated as "Easy," students in the class accused of cheating said the class had become quite difficult, with test questions that were hard to understand. Teaching fellows ran the class discussion groups, graded tests, and often helped students interpret the take-home exam questions. On the final exam, some students admitted they collaborated or committed plagiarism and were forced to withdraw from school. Other students claimed the identical answers, including typos, were due to attending the same sessions with the same teaching fellow.

Exacerbating the situation was the length of time it took to investigate the cheating allegations. Additional staff members were brought in to analyze and color-code specific words on each of the 279 exams. One student under investigation argued that identical answers on his and another student's final exams were due to shared lecture notes, which the administrative board demanded he produce. This demand was made six months after the class ended. The student found some of his notes and was not punished. Through the end of the following fall semester, not all the students knew if they were going to be cleared of allegations or asked to leave. Almost half of those suspected of cheating were athletes.

Leak to the *Harvard Crimson*

Resident deans are Harvard employees who live in undergraduate dorms in order to advise and counsel students. They also have appointments as lecturers and serve on various faculty committees, but they are not tenure track professors. Resident deans are designated as "House Staff," with some faculty privileges.

A resident dean at Harvard has two email accounts: a personal account addressed to their name and a separate administrative account addressed to the post of resident dean for their dormitory, regardless of who may be the resident dean at any given point in time.

Jay Ellison, secretary of the administrative board, sent an email to the administrative accounts of all the resident deans containing guidelines on how to advise athletes who were under investigation for cheating. If a player participated in a single game before being forced to withdraw or placed on probation, the player would lose an entire year of eligibility. Ellison wrote that athletes being investigated should consider whether to complete the fall term and risk a punishment for cheating, or voluntarily take a leave of absence from school and preserve a year of eligibility. On September 10, 2012, Ellison's email was posted online, went viral, and was published in the school newspaper, *The Harvard Crimson,* the next day.

Leak to *IvyGate*

One week later, *IvyGate*, a blog covering Ivy League universities, posted an email from a Harvard student claiming the administrative board had decided on tiered punishments for students involved in the cheating scandal. Citing a conversation with the resident dean, the student said the administrative board's decisions could range from exoneration of students whose similar answers resulted from notes, to a failing course grade and being forced to withdraw from school for students who collaborated on the exam. *The Harvard Crimson* received an almost identical email to the one posted on *IvyGate.*

A spokesperson for the Faculty of Arts and Sciences emailed a denial of the tiered punishment plan and stated decisions would be made on a case-by-case basis. "Every case will be reviewed by the Administrative Board individually and will be resolved in accordance with its ordinary policies and procedures, based on the rules of the faculty and the particular circumstances that pertain to the particular student."

Harvard's First Email Search

Administrators attempted to identify who leaked Ellison's email to the *Harvard Crimson* by asking Sharon Howell, a senior resident dean, "to reach out individually" to the other resident deans to see if anyone would admit to leaking the email. However, her work "yielded no insights." After the *IvyGate* leak, administrators redoubled their efforts to find the source. They said they were concerned "that other information — especially student information we have a duty to protect as private — was at risk [of being leaked]."

According to Harvard's website, administrators are allowed access to faculty email accounts in "extraordinary circumstances such as legal proceedings and internal Harvard investigations." The dean of the Faculty of Arts and Sciences and the Office of the General Counsel must approve any search of faculty email and "the faculty member will be notified [of the search] at the earliest possible opportunity." However, resident deans are classified as staff, not faculty. The staff policy authorizes searching staff emails "at any time" and "for any business purpose" without notifying staff members.

Harvard's information technology (IT) department conducted an email search in September 2012. "A very narrow, careful, and precise subject-line search" was conducted of Ellison's email account and the administrative email accounts of the sixteen resident deans to which Ellison's email was sent. As required, the searches had the approval of Secretary Ellison, the Office of General Counsel, Dean Evelynn Hammonds, and the dean of the Harvard Faculty of Arts & Sciences, Michael Smith. Smith was Evelynn Hammonds's supervisor. Ellison was given advance notice of the searches. The resident deans were not notified.

Harvard IT found one resident dean had forwarded Ellison's email to two student athletes. The resident dean had been advising students who were suspected in the cheating scandal on the options and ramifications of staying enrolled versus leaving school. When the resident dean received the email from Ellison answering the students' questions, she forwarded his email to them.

After speaking with the resident dean, administrators were satisfied that forwarding Ellison's email was "an inadvertent error and not an intentional breach." No action was taken against her. The other resident deans were unaware their email accounts had been searched until six months later, in March 2013, when *The Boston Globe* spoke to Harvard before publishing its article on the email searches. Harvard notified the resident deans just before *The Boston Globe* published the story.

"…I Stand Here to Apologize"

When initially addressing the Harvard faculty, Dean Evelynn Hammonds said only the resident deans' administrative email accounts were examined. Later, she told the faculty she authorized an additional search of the resident deans' personal email accounts as well.

This second investigation looked specifically for the emails leaked to *IvyGate* and *The Harvard Crimson*. Dean Evelynn Hammonds again stated the search was of subject lines only. "Let me be clear: No emails were opened, and no content was searched." The investigation was conducted with the approval of Dean Evelynn Hammonds, Secretary Ellison, and the Office of General Counsel, but without the knowledge of Dean Michael Smith. The second email search proved fruitless. There also appeared to have been at least one other inspection of the resident deans' email accounts, but the record is unclear.

When Hammonds spoke before faculty members about the subsequent email searches that lacked the approval of Dean Michael Smith, she explained, "I and others, entrusted with administering our university business, made serious mistakes, and I stand here to apologize." She regretted not mentioning the additional investigations in prior comments, saying the lapse was caused by her "failure to recollect the additional searches."

"Different Choices Should Have Been Made"

Dean Michael Smith also apologized to the faculty and said unrelated email inspections had been conducted before the cheating incident. He stated email searches happen "very, very rarely. In those rare instances when an email search is authorized, I strongly agree with the community that we should always give notification." Specifically addressing the searches of the resident deans' email accounts, Dean Smith said, "To my great dismay, I cannot stand before you and say definitively what happened in this current case. The records kept are incomplete. And from talking to individuals, I have learned that the memories of specific notifications are meaningfully different." The president of Harvard, Drew Faust, remarked, "Different choices should have been made."

Campus Reaction

Dr. Harry R. Lewis, a professor and former dean of Harvard College, blogged that the email searches would lead him to use his Harvard email account less and his private email account more. Timothy McCarthy, Program Director at Harvard's Kennedy School of Government, posted, "This is disgraceful, even more so than the original cheating scandal, because it involves adults who should know better — really smart, powerful adults, with complete job security." History professor Charles Maier commented, "I think the issue I'm concerned about is that people in a university should not be trolling emails. Even just the subject line — it's considered a kind of searching procedure that we didn't think we worried about at this university."

A student who was exonerated of cheating said searching the resident deans' email accounts may have undermined the privacy administrators claimed they were trying to protect. Emails once believed by students to be confidential communication with their resident deans on sensitive academic and disciplinary issues might now be viewed as compromised and subject to inspection at any time. Summarizing the entire cheating scandal, he said, "I didn't think it could get any more ridiculous."

Now Would Be a Good Time for a Sabbatical

After the email searches were made public by *The Boston Globe*, Dean Evelynn Hammonds, who had been on faculty at Harvard for eleven years, elected to take a yearlong sabbatical. She returned to teach and conduct research after her sabbatical. President Faust said, "We will be fortunate to continue benefiting from her talents and wisdom."

President Faust asked outside attorneys to determine the full extent of the email searches. An internal task force headed by a Harvard law professor will develop guidelines for conducting future email investigations.

...and how to avoid them

An organization's proprietary, internal information is constrained only by an understanding that stakeholders will keep organizational matters within the organization. An implicit component of that compact is that grievances will be redressed in a fair and timely manner and not ignored or repressed. The larger the organization, the larger the outside audience for internal information. If an organization does not listen to its employees, customers, suppliers, and other stakeholders, someone else will.

Technology can reveal when an email was forwarded, by whom, and to whom. A search may detail what happened, but is unlikely to reveal the motivation, thinking, or emotions of the person forwarding an email.

Organizations need to ask and answer several questions before undertaking an email search:

1. Why are emails being forwarded and what can be done to rectify the root cause?

2. What is the organization's policy on searching emails, and how does the organization ensure the policy is followed?

3. What will be done with the information found from the email search?

4. Is the organization willing to weather the adverse publicity if the email search is made public?

Harvard did not appear to ask the question of what motivated its students to forward internal emails to outside sources. College students usually feel a sense of pride in their school, especially one of the most prestigious universities in the world. Why would they forward emails that embarrassed Harvard and, by association, themselves? Their motivation may have included some combination of extreme frustration at the drawn-out process, stressful uncertainty whether they would remain in school, and disenfranchisement from the process. A damaging email forwarded outside the organization is indicative of larger problems within the organization.

"I Should Have Never Sent Them"

The End of Self-Interest

Dewey & LeBoeuf, New York City's largest law firm ever, was built and destroyed in under five years. The firm imploded from incredibly high operating costs of its own making and sharply dropping revenue due to factors beyond its control. Hastening its demise was real-time monitoring of partners' emails and the never-ending pursuit of self-interest.

Recruiting Star Litigators

Steve Davis was the Chairman of LeBoeuf, Lamb, Greene & MacRae, a New York City law firm of 650 attorneys working in the areas of energy, public utilities, and insurance. Stephen DiCarmine, the Executive Director, carried out Davis's decisions, including firings and office closings. Collectively, they were known as "the Steves." In 2004, the Steves felt their firm needed to grow in order to compete with larger law firms that served international corporate clients. They could achieve this growth by merging with another law firm or by raiding other firms for attorneys who would bring their large corporate clients with them. They chose the latter option.

The first attorney the Steves signed was a star securities litigator whose compensation demands included $16 million up front to fund his personal pension and a $1.6 million annual salary not tied to his performance. The firm's investment in the litigator produced terrific returns with one class action lawsuit alone bringing in $40 million to the firm. Additionally, the same litigator landed Royal Dutch Shell, one of the world's largest petroleum companies, as a new client. Over the next ten months, twenty-two new attorneys were brought on as partners, with bonuses and pay guarantees that were kept secret from existing partners to minimize demands for higher salaries. In 2006, *American Lawyer* labeled LeBoeuf, Lamb, Greene & MacRae a "rainmaker magnet."

Alexander Dye was the head of LeBoeuf's compensation committee, a member of the executive committee, and the firm's most powerful attorney aside from Chairman Steve Davis. Dye had built a thriving insurance practice group with the help of other partners and associates.

Dye had a good relationship with Chairman Davis. They traveled together on business to Beijing and Moscow and shared an interest in history. Dye did not like Executive Director DiCarmine, who had no clients but was paid almost $2 million per year. Senior partners implied the executive committee would appoint Dye chairman in 2008, when Davis's five-year term expired. Dye intended to eliminate the executive director and CFO positions and delegate their duties to the other partners while maintaining his own insurance practice.

On a Thursday in March 2007, one day before the executive committee's annual meeting, Chairman Davis came to Dye's office. Davis said he had been talking to members of the executive committee about the following year's chairmanship appointment — and then he dropped the bomb. "They want to reappoint me." Davis asked if both Dye and Schwolsky, Dye's close ally, would support his reappointment. Dye responded, "I'm not going to fight you. You have the votes. But I'm angry."

EWI (Emailing While Intoxicated)

The next night, there was a dinner in the conference room for the executive committee to celebrate Davis's reappointment. After dinner, Dye and Schwolsky went for drinks to Coco Pazzo, an Upper East Side restaurant. That night, and into the early hours of Saturday morning, Dye exchanged a series of emails with Schwolsky. In one email he called Davis a "coward" and "a bad leader who was putting his interest ahead of the firm's." He continued in this vein in another email to Schwolsky.

Dye: "I think many of our colleagues would be surprised to learn that squat, ignorant [expletive deleted] is the kingmaker here...Davis is the bad guy here. I think we need to be opportunistic about how we go after him."

In response, Schwolsky contemplated moving the insurance practice group to another law firm.

Schwolsky: "My only other comment is that we control a lot of business...I think it is really sad that we are being put in a position where we have to take the crown jewel of the firm and put it in play."

By Sunday, Dye had calmed down from Friday night and wrote Chairman Davis a conciliatory email of support.

Dye: "After a weekend of intense introspection... I have decided to put all of this behind me. I will not discuss it again, will be a loyal team player. I will arrive at the office on Monday morning and redouble my efforts to build an even stronger corporate practice. You have my word on that."

However, Dye's angry emails had already surfaced.

Probable Cause

This was not the first instance of Dye misusing email. As head of the firm's compensation committee, Dye knew its decisions were supposed to be confidential. Compensation at law firms is composed of a fixed annual salary plus a year-end bonus. The bonus

an attorney receives is determined by the percentage of the firm's profits allocated to each attorney
by the compensation committee. Dye had broken
this confidentiality previously when he emailed an
attorney at the Washington D.C. office asking why a
member of the compensation committee was trying
to cut the D.C. attorney's bonus. The D.C. attorney,
in turn, expressed his concerns about that member
of the compensation committee to Chairman Davis.
After hearing that Dye had sent confidential information to the D.C. attorney, Davis ordered Stephen
DiCarmine to search the firm's server for all of Dye's
past emails and monitor Dye's emails in real time.

Kicking the Hornet's Nest

Dye suspected that DiCarmine was monitoring his
emails. Yet in emails written over the weekend of the
annual meeting, he added several insults directed
toward DiCarmine.

Dye: "BTW, Steve DiCarmine, if you are reading this,
I'll have your [expletive] head on a stick."

His second email was another threat.

Dye: "Same threat for you DiCarmine…Don't test me."

In a third email, he added a crude sexual suggestion addressed to DiCarmine.

Dye's email rants against Davis, his vulgarities directed toward DiCarmine, and Schwolsky's suggestion of taking the insurance practice to another firm, were all read by Davis within hours of being written. The executive committee held an emergency meeting without Dye on Sunday at 7:30 p.m., forty-eight hours after the dinner celebrating the reappointment of Davis as Chairman. Davis brought in copies of Dye's emails for the committee members to read. An outside law firm read the emails hours earlier and advised that there were ample grounds to fire Dye. Since firing Dye would mean a huge loss in revenue, the executive committee decided to let Dye and Schwolsky stay if they gave up their management positions and titles.

Davis summoned Dye to his office, handed him copies of the emails, and asked, "How could you do this?"

Dye, visibly shaken according to Davis, replied, "I was just sort of showing off to Schwolsky."

Many of the emails were written late at night and Davis questioned, "Were you drinking when you wrote these?"

Dye responded that he was just letting off steam and added, "They were inappropriate, they were dumb, and I should have never sent them." Both Dye and Schwolsky gave up their management positions and stayed with the firm.

That said, Dye was livid because Davis and DiCarmine had read his emails. LeBoeuf's email policy stated that all emails were the property of the firm. Dye had not signed the policy and said he had never been given a copy. After having his emails read and being stripped of his titles and position, Dye was told to sign a copy of the firm's email policy.

Through the Looking Glass

In light of the email threatening to take the insurance practice group to another law firm, Davis felt an urgency to merge with another firm that had a large corporate practice. A few weeks later, in April 2007, a meeting was arranged with Morton Pierce, the Co-Chairman of Dewey Ballantine, a prestigious New York City law firm. Pierce not only managed the firm, but his mergers and acquisitions practice group accounted for almost 10 percent of the firm's revenue.

The offer of a merger could not have come at a better time for Dewey Ballantine. They were riven by the loss of partners and their net income had dropped by 60 percent in the last two years. What was intended for the two firms' mutual benefit resulted in their mutual destruction.

I'll Have What He Had

In discussing a possible merger of their two law firms, Davis told Pierce about the emails from Dye and Schwolsky. Pierce felt Davis handled the matter competently and could run the new firm if they decided to merge. Shortly into the merger discussions, Pierce mentioned that he was familiar with the $16 million signing bonus and $1.6 million annual salary Davis had given the securities litigator only a few years earlier. Pierce asked for a five-year contract with a guaranteed $6 million annual salary, asserting the duration of the commitment would give the new firm credibility. Davis agreed and added a $1 million signing bonus. Davis did not have a contract, but his compensation was $5 million annually.

Davis and Pierce hired McKinsey, a consulting firm, to conduct due diligence for the proposed merger. McKinsey reported that Dewey and LeBoeuf had similar billing rates and no apparent conflicts of interest among its top fifty clients. However, it noted that 5 percent of the partners generated 42 percent of billings and advised, "Create financial incentives for partners to remain at the Firm." In total, about one hundred partners were given contracts with guaranteed salaries and bonuses. Both Dye and Schwolsky received contracts for $3 million per year despite having narrowly avoided being fired for their malicious emails only a few months earlier.

The Bigger They Are…

The merger occurred on October 1, 2007 with the name of the new firm being Dewey & LeBoeuf. The new firm had 1,300 attorneys in twenty-six offices around the world and was the largest in the history of New York City. Its corporate clients included Lloyd's of London, JPMorgan Chase, Disney, Dell, and eBay. In legal circles, some characterized the merger as "Dewey married money, LeBoeuf married up." Only six months after the merger, Davis confidently announced that bonuses would be increased based on a *projected* revenue growth of 10 percent, a growth rate that LeBoeuf had achieved for the previous five years.

A few months after announcing the increase in bonuses, and less than a year after the merger, the financial crisis of 2008 hit. AIG, one of Dewey & LeBoeuf's largest clients, was asking for a government bailout. Merger and acquisition work came to a halt. Instead of a 10 percent increase in revenue in 2008, there was a 20 percent decrease in revenue. When profits decline at law firms, compensation usually does as well. However, Dewey & LeBoeuf had locked itself into contracts promising large compensation packages to more than one hundred partners. The firm met its compensation obligations in 2008 by cutting expenses in 2009 by $100 million. In total, 30 partners, 400 associates, and 450 support personnel were fired. The hope was that as the economy recovered, revenue would rebound to previous levels.

...The Harder They Fall

Unfortunately, toward the end of 2008, Chairman Davis had a larger, more complex problem than meeting the contractually obligated salaries of attorneys, reversing precipitously falling revenue, cutting costs, or making payments to the pension plan that was $80 million in arrears. Dewey & LeBoeuf had a loan from a syndicate of four banks for $100 million containing a covenant requiring the firm show a cash flow of at least $290 million by December 31, 2008. Cash flow is revenue less operating expenses. Law firms generate revenue through billing clients, and billings were down by $200 million in 2008. The firm was $50 million short on the cash flow needed to satisfy its loan.

In a series of email exchanges, the collective pressure on senior management to somehow meet the cash flow requirement of $290 million in the remaining twenty-seven days in 2008 was palpable. The two primary financial administrators were Chief Financial Officer Joel Sanders and Director of Finance Francis Canellas. The overarching constraint was that, with only three weeks until Christmas, neither expenses nor revenue could be significantly decreased or increased by the end of the year.

On December 4, 2008, CFO Sanders emailed Director Canellas.

CFO Sanders: "What revenue number must we hit not to breach our [loan] covenants?"

Director of Finance Canellas: "The agreement call [sic] for Cash Flow of 290M. Hence we need 994M in Revenue to be in compliance."

Later that same day, CFO Sanders emailed the firm's Chief Operating Officer complaining that someone had purchased IT equipment costing over a million dollars without the approval of the Finance department.

CFO Sanders: "I don't know anything about [the IT contract] and I don't want to cook the books anymore. We need to stop doing that."

With only eight days to satisfy the loan requirement, CFO Sanders wrote Chairman Davis on December 23, 2008.

CFO Sanders: "The banks will pull our [credit] lines in a heartbeat if we don't satisfy our covenants."

By December 30, 2008, the firm was one day away from violating its cash flow covenant and being forced to repay the entire $100 million loan. CFO Sanders emailed Chairman Davis and Executive Director DiCarmine on the need for an additional $50 million in revenue, which would be impossible to generate the day before New Year's Eve.

CFO Sanders: "50M [in collections] tomorrow to meet our [loan] covenant."

Chairman Davis: "Ugh."

Rather than going public with the drop in cash flow and talking to its bankers, the SEC alleged that the firm developed a strategy for misclassifying expenses, reimbursements, and partners' capital contributions as revenue. The reclassifications were tracked in a detailed spreadsheet entitled the "Master Plan," which was created by Director of Finance Canellas. The spreadsheet listed the actual profits, the amount needed to meet the firm's cash flow requirement, and what misclassifications were needed in order to give the appearance of cash flow of $290 million.

On the last day of 2008, both CFO Sanders and Director of Finance Canellas worked with a young collections manager who was promised his full bonus if the firm met its obligations by implementing the Master Plan. By the close of business on December 31, 2008, $50 million in reclassifications had added a specious $50 million to cash flow. The collections manager sent a congratulatory email to Canellas.

Collections manager, subject line: "Great job dude. We kicked ass! Time to get paid."

Collections manager, body of email: "Hey man, I don't know where you come up with some of this stuff [reclassifications], but you saved the day. It's been a rough year but it's been damn good. Nice work dude. Let's get paid!"

"Live With It"

Revenue continued to drop in 2009, sparking another crisis in the first part of 2010. This time, the crisis revolved around employee compensation. Dewey & LeBoeuf was contractually obligated to pay $240 million in year end bonuses to its partners by the end of January 2010, but only had $119 million available. Foreseeing a shortfall, the question of whether bonuses should be paid to those without contracts was addressed at the 2009 annual meeting. Pierce, with his guaranteed $6 million annual salary, vocally opposed paying bonuses to employees without contracts. "Tell people, 'Sorry, this is what you earned. Live with it. It's a good living.'" The lack of cash for bonuses and the impact of previous accounting machinations were reflected in an email from CFO Sanders to Davis, DiCarmine, and others.

CFO Sanders: "Keep in mind though that at these levels [of income] we will not have the cash to pay the partners by Jan 31 [2010] since $25M is fake income."

Instead of obtaining another bank loan to pay the bonuses, the firm issued $150 million in bonds, which were purchased by thirteen insurance companies based on Dewey & LeBoeuf's financial statements from 2008 and 2009.

We're Just Talking

In the summer of 2010, a recruiter told Chairman Davis that Pierce was negotiating an $8 million contract with another large law firm. Davis was irate and had DiCarmine read Pierce's emails. DiCarmine discovered that Pierce was actually in contract negotiations with not one, but three other law firms.

When Davis confronted Pierce about the emails, Pierce replied, "I'm just talking to people." Pierce's billing revenue had dropped by half since the start of the financial crisis in October 2008. DiCarmine wanted to fire Pierce, but the other partners did not think they could afford to lose him with revenue being down so drastically. In order to keep him, Davis increased Pierce's contract by $2 million to $8 million per year. Word of Pierce's new contract spread throughout the firm. Soon other partners, and in some cases entire practice groups, came to Davis demanding to renegotiate their compensation contracts.

The Beginning of the End

In the fall of 2011, Davis learned the banks would not renew Dewey & LeBoeuf's $100 million loan, which was coming due in April 2012. The ongoing drop in revenue combined with the loss of its bank loan proved more than the firm could withstand. Davis started asking partners to defer their 2011 year-end bonuses, but the contract with Pierce put Davis in a quandary. Pierce's contract contained a clause that accelerated the entire $40 million due him if his year-end bonus was not paid. On January 31, 2012, Davis sent Pierce an email suggesting they meet with DiCarmine that Friday. Pierce was concerned about being paid his bonus.

Pierce: "Fine. I'm due $5.5 million. Will I be getting that amount today?"

Davis: "We're being very conservative on managing our cash and probably can't get it out today. We're looking at the situation on a daily basis and will keep you updated."

Pierce proceeded to Davis's office where Davis told him, "We're thinking of ways to work this out."

Pierce asked, "What ways?"

"We haven't come up with anything," answered Davis. Pierce returned to his office and wrote Davis another email.

Pierce: "This email constitutes notice of failure to pay base compensation."

Outside counsel retained by Pierce wrote a letter demanding the firm pay $40 million dollars within thirty days, as contractually obligated.

Allegations and Investigations

Concurrent to the exchange with Pierce, a group of partners from Dewey & LeBoeuf approached the Manhattan District Attorney's office and outlined its allegations regarding the firm's accounting practices. The SEC opened an investigation because the $150 million bond offering relied on potentially misleading financial statements, which would constitute a violation of securities regulations. Investigations by the SEC and the Manhattan District Attorney's office led to massive partner defections.

In March 2012, Dye and Schwolsky took the insurance practice group to another law firm. In the first week of May 2012, Pierce left the firm along with seventy other attorneys. On May 28, 2012, Dewey & LeBoeuf filed for bankruptcy protection, citing creditors' claims of over half a billion dollars. Theirs was the largest law firm bankruptcy case to date.

After two years of investigations, criminal and civil charges were brought against Davis, DiCarmine, Sanders, and Canellas in March 2014. They were brought up on almost 150 criminal counts, including grand larceny and scheme to defraud. If convicted of the criminal charges, each faced prison sentences ranging from eight to twenty-five years. Both the D.A. and the SEC cases made extensive use of the emails exchanged between the four men.

The five-month trial concluded in December 2015. The jury deliberated for twenty-two days and acquitted the defendants of dozens of counts of falsifying business records. The jury remained hung on the major charges. After the jury announced its verdict, the Assistant D.A. said there would be a retrial. It is estimated that legal fees for the defendants were in the millions of dollars.

...and how to avoid them

Emails are written snapshots capturing the thoughts and feelings of the writer at a specific point in time. Alexander Dye's rash, rage-filled vitriol revealed anger, frustration, and a sense of betrayal at not being named Chairman. Had Dye been ranting at the end of a bar instead of writing an email, it is questionable whether anyone would have paid attention to him. Since Davis and DiCarmine elected to monitor his emails, the firm had an obligation to address Dye's threats and hate speech. The written word imparts a gravitas the spoken word lacks. The underlying assumption is that time and thought have been expended on what was written, even if that is not the case.

Besides Dye's personal attacks, there was the issue of Schwolsky's suggestion to move the insurance practice group. In an information-dense society, parsing relevant information from the insubstantial, especially in emotion-laden content, can be complicated. Signal-to-noise ratio is the proportion of useful information in relation to all information collected. Consistency over time validates a signal. Human Resources departments evaluate employees' performances over years, so decisions are not usually based on one incident, but the person's behavior as a whole. Over the course of years, Dye had proven himself to be a loyal, productive member of the firm, which is why he was seriously considered to be Chairman.

The sudden noise of a loud thunderclap can be frightening, but is harmless. The decision by Davis and DiCarmine to merge with Dewey was driven by fear from one comment in one late night email, despite Dye's email on Sunday night reaffirming his commitment to the firm. Davis and DiCarmine, out of fear, confused noise for signal and traded loyalty for greed.

Rushing into a merger as a result of monitoring Dye's email, Davis and DiCarmine again elected to monitor a partner's emails. Again, they acted out of fear by matching Pierce's negotiations for an $8 million salary, a concession that compounded their financial difficulties and hastened the firm's demise.

Conclusions

No Experience Required

At age sixteen, a person is allowed to navigate a 5,000-pound vehicle traveling seventy-five miles per hour at night in the rain. Driver's Education courses are available to teach the skills needed in driving and a learner's permit provides a hands-on training period for instruction and supervision. Earning the right to drive independently requires demonstrated competency by passing a government-mandated written exam and a driving test.

In spite of extensive training, fatal accidents are almost three times higher for drivers ages sixteen to nineteen than for twenty-year-olds. It simply takes years to master the complexities required to drive safely in an inherently dangerous environment. A transient lapse in awareness of one's relationship to other vehicles can result in a crash.

Many children have cellphones and email accounts in elementary school. At age thirteen, an adolescent may create a social media account and start building a personal, intimate, online portrait of themselves half a decade before high school graduation and a decade before graduating college and starting a career. No training, supervision, or demonstration of competency is required. Adults aware of potentially catastrophic outcomes from driving seem to lack the same awareness for their offspring and themselves in regard to electronic communication.

A car crash at seventy-five miles an hour results in glass and steel strewn about the roadway. Emergency workers attend to injured drivers, passengers, and bystanders, and removal of the wreckage. An electronic communication wreck lacks the visual drama, but imparts damage just as real and just as permanent. A momentary lapse in judgment may prove catastrophic for the writer, their family, coworkers, and stakeholders.

Access Equals Power

Emails, texts, and social media promise the writer the power to be heard. The resources and blood expended to gain and retain power throughout history is extraordinary and continues unabated. In a society where relinquishing control is viewed as weakness, power is relinquished through every message sent without forethought given to the potential consequences.

Many people have an inaccurate perception of their ability to manage electronic communication well. Specifically, individuals underestimate the power of their words to profoundly change the attitudes of others toward them. Every posting, message, or email creates an impression, a public persona, from which people make judgments. We make judgments about others, but how often do we turn that critical analysis on ourselves?

While this is one way we cede power to others using electronic communication, it is not the most significant. Once a message is sent electronically, the writer has ceded power not just to the recipient, but to whomever the recipient chooses to forward the information. To access electronic communication is to control it. The recipient, not the writer, has power over future dissemination of the writer's words. How often do we reread what we have written and attempt to view it through the eyes of another? How much more carefully would we choose our words if we fully grasped the magnitude of the power we are giving the recipient?

Neither inherently good nor evil, electronic communication platforms are 100 percent dependent on user input. There is not a story in this book about a person's life or a company's future being upended by technology. Upheaval came from words written on a blank screen. Mindful use of these electronic platforms enables more efficient communication, faster decision-making, and can positively impact millions of lives, as seen in the Arab Spring of 2011. Their power and potential should command our respect in order to reap their benefits while avoiding their pitfalls.

BIBLIOGRAPHY

Introduction

Crash Following Loss of Engine Power Due to Fuel Exhaustion, Air Methods Corporation Eurocopter AS350 B2, N352LN, National Transportation Safety Board, http://www.ntsb. gov/investigations/AccidentReports/Pages/AAR1302. aspx

Bryan Tau, "Hillary Clinton Interviewed by FBI in Email Probe" *The Wall Street Journal,* July 2, 2016, http://www.wsj.com/ articles/hillary-clinton-interviewed-by-fbi-1467478221

Kate O'Keefe and Byron Tau, "FBI Won't Recommend Hillary Clinton be Indicted Over Private Email Use," *The Wall Street Journal,* July 5, 2016, http://www.wsj.com/articles/ fbi-won-t-recommend-clinton-be-indicted-over-private-email-use-1467731774

Bryan Tau, "Clinton Emails: 5 Revelations From the Watchdog Report," *The Wall Street Journal,* May 25, 2016, http:// blogs.wsj.com/washwire/2016/05/25/clinton-emails-5-revelations-from-the-watchdog-report/

Gone, but not forgotten

Bethany McLean and Peter Elkind, *The Smartest Guys the Room*, Penguin Group, 2003.

Stephen M. Bainbridge, *The Complete Guide to Sarbanes-Oxley*, Adams Business, 2007

Jill Gilbert Welytok, JD, CPA, *Sarbanes-Oxley for Dummies*, Second edition, Wiley Publishing, 2008

J.G. Kritikson, Sr. Director of Business & Regulatory Affairs, CalPX, January 28, 2000 "California Electricity Market Primer," Prepared for CalPX Board of Governors, "Enron traders caught on tape," CBS News June 1, 2004
http://www.cbsnews.com/news/enron-traders-caught-on-tape/

"The Western Energy Crisis, the Enron Bankruptcy, and FERC's Response," https://www.ferc.gov/industries/electric/indus-act/wec/chron/chronology.pdf

"Transmission Utilization Group: COI Utilization Report," May 04, 2011
http://www.oatioasis.com/WASN/WASNdocs/COI_Utilization_Report_S.Anners.pdf

"Synopsis of the Energy Policy Act of 1992: New Tasks for State Utility Commissions

The National Regulatory Research Institute," The Ohio State University, http://www.ipu.msu.edu/library/pdfs/ nrri/Costello-Energy-Policy-Act-93-7-June-93.pdf

Robert McCullough "Congestion Manipulation in ISO California," Memorandum

https://www.bpa.gov/power/lp/sn03/files/Parties_ Testimony_Rebuttal/SN-03-E-CR&YA-02X.pdf

"Promoting Wholesale Competition Through Open Access Non-discriminatory Transmission Services by Public Utilities; Recovery of Stranded Costs by Public Utilities and Transmitting Utilities," A rule by the Federal Energy Regulatory Commission on 5-10/1996.

https://www.federalregister.gov/articles/1996/ 05/10/96-10694/promoting-wholesale-competition- through-open-access-non--discriminatory-transmission- services-by

"California's Electricity Situation Briefing for the staff of the U.S. House of Representatives," Energy Information Administration, February 9, 2001

Paul L. Jaskow, Massachusetts Institute of Technology, "California's Electricity Crisis," *Oxford Review of Economic Policy*, Vol. 17, Number 3
http://economics.mit.edu/files/1149

James L Sweeney, "The California Electricity Crisis," April 9, 2002, http://web.stanford.edu/~jsweeney/paper/Lessons%20 for%20the%20Future.pdf

From: Christian Yoder and Stephen Hall, To: Richard Sanders, Confidential Attorney/Client Work Product Memorandum, "Traders' Strategies in the California Wholesale Power Market/ISO Sanctions," December 6, 2000

Senate Hearing 107-854, "Asleep at the switch: FERC's oversight of Enron Corporation — Vol. I, Hearing before the Committee on Government Affairs United States Senate One Hundred Seventh Congress Second Session," November 12, 2002
http://www.gpo.gov/fdsys/pkg/CHRG-107shrg83483/ html/CHRG-107shrg83483.htm

David Barboza, "How Enron bet on energy crisis/Huge profit taken as traders shuffled gas, electricity," *SFGate*, December 12, 2002, http://www.sfgate.com/crime/article/How-Enron-bet-on-energy-crisis-Huge-profit-2746583.php

NOW, *PBS.com*, http://www.pbs.org/now/transcript/transcriptNOW132_full.html

"Follow the Enron Money," *CBSNEWS.COM*, January 12, 2002, http://www.cbsnews.com/news/follow-the-enron-money/

Charles Wilbanks, Ex Enron CEO to leave prison early, *MoneyWatch*, June 21, 2013, http://www.cbsnews.com/news/ex-enron-ceo -jeff-skilling-to-leave-prison-early/

Timeline: A chronology of Enron Corp, *New York Times*, January 18, 2006, http://www.nytimes.com/2006/01/18/business/worldbusiness/18iht-web.0117enron.time.html?pagewanted=all&_r=0

Jef Feeley, "Takeda Jury Can Hear Claims Over Destroyed Actos Files," *Bloomberg Business*, January 29, 2014, http://www.bloomberg.com/news/articles/2014-01-30/takeda-jury-can-hear-claims-over-destroyed-actos-files

John McKinnon, "New Information Deepens the Mystery of the Missing IRS Emails," *The Wall Street Journal*, July 21, 2014, http://blogs.wsj.com/washwire/2014/07/21/new-information-deepens-the-mystery-of-the-missing-irs-emails/

John McKinnon, "Hunt for Missing IRS Emails Resumes," *The Wall Street Journal*, July 23, 2014, http://www.wsj.com/articles/hunt-for-missing-irs-emails-resumes-1406152329

John D. McKinnon, "GOP Says Lerner Email Shows Bias Against Conservatives," *The Wall Street Journal*, July 30, 2014, http://www.wsj.com/articles/gop-says-lerner-email-shows-bias-against-conservatives-1406739923

John D. McKinnon, "Former IRS Official's Email Lost When Backup Tapes Routinely Erased," *The Wall Street Journal*, June 25, 2015, http://www.wsj.com/articles/former-irs-officials-email-lost-when-backup-tapes-routinely-erased-1435234390?tesla=y

Line upon line

CV13-00779, United States of America v. McGraw-Hill Companies, Inc., and Standard and Poor's Financial Services LLC, Central District Court of California, http://graphics8.nytimes.com/packages/pdf/business/09dealbook-henning.pdf

Bradley Hope, "Bear Stearns Liquidators Sue Fitch, Moody's, S&P Suit Accuses Firms of Misleading Investors on Ratings Quality" *The Wall Street Journal*, November 11, 2013, http://www.wsj.com/articles/SB10001424052702303914304579192343147508158

Peter Coy, "Bill Clinton's drive to increase homeownership went way too far," *Bloomberg Business*, February 27, 2008, http://www.businessweek.com/the_thread/hotproperty/archives/2008/02/clintons_drive.html

"The Enduring Ratings Racket: Regulators sue the credit raters whose profit margins they guarantee" *The Wall Street Journal*, December 6, 2013, http://www.wsj.com/articles/SB10001424052702303497804579238421860147210

Kevin Johnson and Kevin McCoy, "Feds: S&P defrauded investors, fueled crisis," *USA Today*, February 5, 2013, http://www.usatoday.com/story/money/business/2013/02/05/justice-states-sue-sp/1892647/

Carol D. Leonnig, "How HUD Mortgage Policy Fed The Crisis," *The Washington Post* June 10, 2008, http://www.washingtonpost.com/wp-dyn/content/article/2008/06/09/AR2008060902626.html

"Richard Vedder and Christopher Denhart: How the College Bubble Will Pop," *The Wall Street Journal*, January 8, 2014, http://www.wsj.com/articles/SB10001424052702303933104 579302951214561682

Timothy Martin, "Ratings Firms Ride Bond Resurgence, S&P, Moody's Expected to Post Record Profits," *The Wall Street Journal*, April 23, 2014, http://www.wsj.com/articles/SB10 00142405270230478840457951979410492327 8

Timothy Martin, "Justice Department Investigating Moody's Investors Service
Probe Looking Into Favorable Ratings on Mortgage Bonds Before the Financial Crisis," *The Wall Street Journal*, February1, 2015, http://www.wsj.com/articles/ justice-department-investigating-moodys-investors-service-1422822296

Timothy Martin, "S&P Near $1.37 Billion Settlement of Crisis-Era Suits
Deal Is Expected to be Announced as Early as Thursday," *The Wall Street Journal* January 28, 2015, http://www.wsj.com/articles/s-p-justice-department-states-close-to-1-37-billion-settlement-1422460397

Timothy W. Martin and Andrew Grossman, "How the Justice Department, S&P Came to Terms," *The Wall Street Journal*, February 2, 2015, http://www.wsj.com/articles/s-p-pact-hinged-on-trade-offs-with-justice-1422915828

Matt Taibbi, "The Last Mystery of the Financial Crisis," *Rolling Stone*, June 19, 2013, http://www.rollingstone.com/politics/news/the-last-mystery-of-the-financial-crisis-20130619

Timothy W. Martin, "S&P Nears Settlement on Real-Estate Bond Ratings," *The Wall Street Journal*, December 25, 2014, http://www.wsj.com/articles/s-p-nears-settlement-on-real-estate-bond-ratings-1419555235

Andrew Ackerman, "SEC Faults Rating Firms for Rule Lapses, Lax Cybersecurity Reports Says Some Firms Lack Sufficient Internal Systems to Prevent 'Misuse, Inappropriate Dissemination," *The Wall Street Journal*, December 24, 2014, http://www.wsj.com/articles/sec-faults-credit-rating-firms-for-rule-lapses-lax-cybersecurity-1419433389

Timothy W. Martin, "SEC Is Gearing Up to Focus on Ratings Firms," *The Wall Street Journal*, June 25, 2014, http://www.wsj.com/articles/sec-is-gearing-up-to-focus-on-ratings-firms-1403651968

Jeannete Neuman, Evans Perez, and Jean Eaglesham, "U.S., S&P Settle In for Bitter Combat" *The Wall Street Journal*, February 6, 2013, http://www.wsj.com/articles/SB100014 24127887324445904578285802822704578

Joe Palazzolo, "Back from the Dead: A Law Called FIRREA," *The Wall Street Journal*, February 5, 2013, http://blogs. wsj.com/law/2013/02/05/back-from-the-dead-a-law-called-firrea/

Jacob Gershman, "Sitting in the Hot Seat While Sitting In Judgment," *The Wall Street Journal*, February 5, 2013, http://blogs.wsj.com/law/2013/02/05/sitting-in-the-hot-seat-while-sitting-in-judgment/

David Benoit and Jeannette Neumann, "US v S&P: Talking Heads and Highlights From the Suit," *The Wall Street Journal*, February 5, 2013, http://blogs.wsj.com/law/2013/02/05/us-v-sp-talking-heads-and-highlights-from-the-suit/

David Reilly, "Putting Rating Firms on Negative Watch," *The Wall Street Journal*, February 4, 2013, http://www.wsj.com/articles/SB10001424127887324445904578284422374800586

Michael R. Crittenden, "Democratic Lawmakers Praise S&P Lawsuit," *The Wall Street Journal*, February 5, 2013, http://blogs.wsj.com/washwire/2013/02/05/democratic-lawmakers-praise-sp-lawsuit/

Steven Russolill, "McGraw-Hill Shares Slump Again: 'Headline Risk Rears Ugly Head'" *The Wall Street Journal*, February 5, 2013, http://blogs.wsj.com/marketbeat/2013/02/05/mcgraw-hill-shares-slump-again-headline-risk-rears-ugly-head/

Jeannette Neumann, "Shifting Blame Muddles S&P Suit," *The Wall Street Journal*, February 14, 2013, http://www.wsj.com/articles/SB10001424127887324432004578304323408292716?mod=_newsreel_5

Jean Englesham, Jeannette Neumann, and Evan Perez, "U.S. Sues S&P Over Ratings," *The Wall Street Journal*, February 5, 2013, http://www.wsj.com/articles/SB10001424127887324445904578284064003795142

Jeannette Neumann, "U.S. Backs States in Jurisdiction Dispute With S&P," *The Wall Street Journal*, March 29, 2013, http://www.wsj.com/articles/SB1000142412788732400070457839073004103031

Jeannette Neumann, "Big Question in U.S. vs. S&P," *The Wall Street Journal*, April 7, 2013, http://www.wsj.com/articles/SB10001424127887323550604578408823708827896

Jeannette Neumann, Serena Ng, and Aaron Lucchetti, "At S&P, a Crusader for Tough Ratings," *The Wall Street Journal*, October 5, 2011, http://www.wsj.com/articles/SB10001424052970204138204576598822458842368

Tom Lauricella and Matt Phillips, "Downgrade Threat Looms: U.S. Could Lose Top Rating; Obama Issues Stark Warning as Boehner Slams Spending," *The Wall Street Journal*, July 26, 2011, http://www.wsj.com/articles/SB10001424053111903999904576468553582790160

Alan Zibel and Tess Stynes, "S&P Cuts U.S. Government Entities," *The Wall Street Journal*, Aug. 8, 2011, http://www.wsj.com/articles/SB10001424053111904007304576496160975791624

Damian Paletta and E.S. Browning, "U.S. Warned on Debt Load: S&P Signals Top Credit Rating Is in Danger, Stoking Political Battle on Deficit," *The Wall Street Journal*, April 19, 2011, http://www.wsj.com/articles/SB10001424052748704004004576270693061767996

"S&P Downgrades U.S. Debt Rating — Press Release" August 5, 2011, http://blogs.wsj.com/marketbeat/2011/08/05/sp-downgrades-u-s-debt-rating-press-release/

"Standard & Poor's Says DOJ Civil Lawsuit Is Unjustified And Without Legal Merit" February 5, 2013 /PRNewswire-First-Call, http://investor.mcgraw-hill.com/phoenix.zhtml?c=96562&p=irol-newsArticle&ID=1781608

An email ignored

Andrew Grossman, Christina Rexrode, and Dan Fitzpatrick, "Behind the Scenes of Citigroup's $7 Billion Settlement," *The Wall Street Journal*, July 13, 2014, http://www.wsj.com/articles/behind-the-scenes-of-citigroups-7-billion-settlement-1405274009

Madlen Read, "Citi Loses Almost $10B, Slashes Dividend" Huffington Post, January 15, 2008, http://www.huffingtonpost.com/huff-wires/ 20080115/citigroup/

Andrew Grossman, Christina Rexrode, and Dan Fitzpatrick, "Citigroup Nears Deal to Resolve Mortgage Probe" *The Wall Street Journal*, July 8, 2014, http://www.wsj.com/

articles/u-s-citi-near-multi-billion-dollar-deal-to-resolve-mortgage-probe-1404851868

Jonathan Stempel and Dan Wilchins, "Citigroup shares slide despite Alwaleed move," *Reuters,* November 20, 2008, http://www.reuters.com/article/2008/11/20/us-citigroup-idUSTRE4AJ45G20081120

Christina Rexrode and Andrew Grossman, "Citigroup to Pay $7 Billion to Resolve Mortgage Probe," *The Wall Street Journal,* July 14, 2014, http://www.wsj.com/articles/citigroup-to-pay-7-billion-to-resolve-mortgage-probe-1405335864

Devlin Barrett and Christina Rexrode, "U.S. Tells Citi to Raise Mortgage Settlement Offer," *The Wall Street Journal,* June 13, 2014, http://www.wsj.com/articles/u-s-to-file-suit-against-citi-if-it-doesnt-raise-offer-to-settle-probe-1402674315

Andrew Grossan, Emily Glazer and Christina Rexrode, "How a Memo Cost Big Banks $37 Billion: Justice Department Lawyer Jump-Started Probe That Led to Three Giant Settlements," *The Wall Street Journal,* December 21, 2014, http://www.wsj.com/articles/how-a-memo-cost-big-banks-37-billion-1418959802

Gregory Zuckerman, *The Greatest Trade Ever*, Broadway Business. 2009 *PBS Frontline*, "Untouchable," http://www.pbs.org/wgbh/pages/frontline/business-economy-financial-crisis/untouchables/transcript-37/

Citigroup's 2007, 2008, 2009, 2010, 2011, 2012, and 2013 Annual Reports

"Financial Crisis Inquiry Commission," January 13, 2010, 1100 Longworth House Office Building, Washington, District of Columbia, http://docslide.us/embed/2010-0113-transcript.html

Testimony of Richard M. Bowen, III, Presented to the Financial Crisis Inquiry Commission, "Hearing on Subprime Lending And Securitization And Government Sponsored Enterprises," April 7, 2010, http://fcic.law.stanford.edu/hearings/testimony/subprime-lending-and-securitization-and-enterprises

Testimony of Richard M. Bowen before the Financial Crisis Inquiry Commission Hearing on Subprime Lending And Securitization And Government Sponsored Enterprises, April 7, 2010, http://hereisthecity.com/en-gb/2010/04/08/testimony_of_richard_m_bowen_iii/

Pandora's box

Ted Mann and Josh Dawsey, "After New Jersey Bridge Scandal, Two Lives Veer Off Course," *The Wall Street Journal,* September 18, 2016, http://www.wsj.com/articles/after-new-jersey-bridge-scandal-two-lives-veer-off-course-1474209111

Ned Levin, "J.P. Morgan Hired 222 Friends, Family of Leaders at 75% of Major Chinese Firms It Took Public in Hong Kong," *The Wall Street Journal,* November 30, 2015, http://www.wsj.com/articles/j-p-morgan-hires-were-referred-by-china-ipo-clients-1448910715

Ned Levin, "J.P. Morgan Hires Were Referred by China IPO Clients
Bank employed friends and family of executives at three-fourths of the major Chinese firms it took public in Hong Kong," *The Wall Street Journal,* November 30, 2015 http://www.wsj.com/articles/j-p-morgan-hires-were-referred-by-china-ipo-clients-1448910715

Edna Curran and Ned Levine, "Banks Angling for China IPO Hired a CEO's Daughter," *The Wall Street Journal* August 1, 2014, http://www.wsj.com/articles/banks-angling-for-china-ipo-hired-a-ceos-daughter-1406910827

Eric Lipton, "Before Oct. 1, a Scramble to Fix Health Site" *The New York Times,* November 21, 2013, http://www.nytimes.com/2013/11/22/us/politics/before-oct-1-a-scramble-to-fix-health-site.html

Ted Mann and Heather Haddon, "Bridge-Spat Emails Pose Questions For Christie," *The Wall Street Journal,* January 9, 2014, http://www.wsj.com/articles/SB10001424052702303393804579308331794186904

Ted Mann and Heather Hadron, "Bridge Jam's Cause a Mystery," *The Wall Street Journal,* September 17, 2013, http://www.wsj.com/articles/SB10001424127887324665604579081630876156774

Lisa Fleisher, Ted Mann, and Neil King Jr., "Chris Christie Moves to Contain Fallout From Bridge Scandal," *The Wall Street Journal,* January 9, 2014, http://www.wsj.com/articles/SB10001424052702304347904579310313594568996

Ted Mann, "George Washington Bridge Jam Began With Phone Call People Familiar With the Matter Pinpoint a Cause for Traffic Tie-up," *The Wall Street Journal,* November 7, 2013, http://www.wsj.com/articles/SB10001424052702304448204579184030525950894

Ned Levin, Emily Glazer and Christopher M. Matthews, "In J.P. Morgan Emails, a Tale of China and Connections," *The Wall Street Journal,* February 6, 2015, http://www.wsj.com/articles/in-j-p-morgan-emails-a-tale-of-china-and-connections-1423241289

Emily Glazer, Dan Fitzpatrick and Jean Eaglesham, "J.P. Morgan Knew of China Hiring Concerns Before Probe," *The Wall Street Journal,* October 23, 2014, http://www.wsj.com/articles/j-p-morgan-was-aware-of-overseas-hiring-concerns-before-u-s-probe-1413998056

Ted Mann and Heather Haddon, "Lawmakers Seek Subpoenas in George Washington Bridge Investigation," *The Wall Street Journal,* October 17, 2013, http://blogs.wsj.com/metropolis/2013/10/17/lawmakers-seek-subpoenas-in-george-washington-bridge-investigation/

Jessica Silver-Greenberg and Ben Protess, "J.P. Morgan Hiring Put China's Elite on an Easy Track, *The Wall Street Journal,* August 29, 2013, http://dealbook.nytimes.com/2013/08/29/jpmorgan-hiring-put-chinas-elite-on-an-easy-track/

Ted Mann and Heather Haddon, "N.J. Lawmakers Release New Bridge Lane Closure Records," *The Wall Street Journal,* January 10, 2014, http://www.wsj.com/articles/SB100014 24052702303393804579312242273288288

Robert Pear and Eric Lipton, "Health Website Official Tells of White House Briefings," *The New York Times,* November 13, 2013, http://www.nytimes.com/2013/11/14/us/ officials-say-they-dont-know-cost-of-health-website-fixes. html

Eric Lipton, "Health Site Infighting Detailed in Emails," *The New York Times,* November 15, 2013, http://www.nytimes. com/2013/11/16/us/health-site-infighting-detailed-in-emails.html

Peter Nicholas and Carol E. Lee, "White House Soul-Searches as Errors Mount," *The Wall Street Journal,* November 17, 2013, http://www.wsj.com/articles/SB1000142405270230 35595045792003604351878816

Sarah Palin, "The Palin E-Mails, 24,000 organized by topics," *The New York Times,* June 10, 2011, http://projects.nytimes. com/palin-emails

Ted Mann, "Port Chief Fumed Over Bridge Jam," *The Wall Street Journal,* October 1, 2013, http://www.wsj.com/articles/SB10001424052702304373104579109860563887326

Jennifer Rubin, "The worst excuse ever: The Rhodes memo debacle" *The Washington Post,* May 1, 2014, http://www.washingtonpost.com/blogs/right-turn/wp/2014/05/01/the-worst-excuse-ever-the-rhodes-memo-debacle/

Dan Fitzpatrick, Enda Curran, and Justin Baer, "J.P. Morgan Emails Note Hire's Family Ties," *The Wall Street Journal,* December 8, 2013, http://www.wsj.com/articles/SB10001424052702303560204579246674206332380

Emily Galzer, Michael Rothfeld, and Christopher M. Matthews, "Two J. P. Morgan Executives Connected to Asia Hiring Probe Pushed Out," *The Wall Street Journal,* February 12, 2015, http://www.wsj.com/articles/two-j-p-morgan-executives-connected-to-asia-hiring-probe-pushed-out-1423788737

Emails from top Gov, Christie aides on lane closure, http://dng.northjersey.com/media_server/tr/2014/01/09gwb/port_authority_2014.pdf

Per our conversation

John D. Stoll, "Apple Sued for Poaching A123 Employees" *The Wall Street Journal*, February 19, 2015, http://www.wsj.com/articles/apple-sued-for-poaching-a123-employees-1424325473

Maureen Farrell, "Facebook: How to Spend $19 Billion in 11 Days," *The Wall Street Journal*, April 19, 2014, http://blogs.wsj.com/moneybeat/2014/02/19/facebook-how-to-spend-19-billion-in-11-days/

Reed Albergotti, Doug MacMillian, and George Stahl, "Facebook Investors Shrug Off Concerns About $19 Billion Deal Shares Rise as WhatsApp Buy Is Seen Helping Social Network's Mobile, International Operations," *The Wall Street Journal*, February 20, 2014, http://www.wsj.com/articles/SB100014240527023037755045793948121 38707896

Alistair Barr, "Silicon Valley Pay Settlement Gets Tentative OK," *The Wall Street Journal*, March 4, 2015, http://www.wsj.com/articles/silicon-valley-wage-settlement-gets-tentative-ok-1425495682

Heather Somerville, "Silicon Valley tech companies reap record-level investments" *Bay Area News*, April 18, 2014, http://www.mercurynews.com/business/ci_25590584/valley-companies-reap-record-level-investments

Jeff Elder, "Silicon Valley Tech Giants Struck Deals on Hiring, Say Documents" *The Wall Street Journal*, April 20, 2014, http://www.wsj.com/articles/SB10001424052702304626304579509700352730842

Case5:11-cv-02509-LHK, Exhibit 250, Email From: Eric Schmidt at Google, To: Steve Jobs at Apple, Subject: Google recruiters calling Apple – isolated incident, Date: March 9, 2007

Jeff Elder, "Judge Clears Way for Trial in Silicon Valley Wage Case," *The Wall Street Journal*, March, 28, 2014, http://blogs.wsj.com/digits/2014/03/28/judge-clears-way-for-trial-in-silicon-valley-wage-case/

Case 5:11-cv-02509-LHK, Order denying defendants' individual motions for summary judgment, In RE: High-tech employee antitrust litigation, United States District Court Northern District of California San Jose Division, http://www.lieffcabraser.com/Documents/htcc-order-denying-summary-judgment-20140328.pdf

Case 5:11-cv-02509-LHK, Exhibit 666 to Cisneros declaration in support of plaintiffs' supplemental motion for class [ECF NO. 418-2] redacted version, http://online.wsj.com/public/resources/documents/sandberg.pdf

Case 5:11-cv-02509-LHK, Exhibit 660 to CISNEROS declaration redacted version, http://online.wsj.com/public/resources/documents/sergey.pdf

Breathe. Think. Reply.

Center for Responsive Politics, https://www.opensecrets.org/lobby/index.php, data on number of lobbyists and funding of same.

Brody Mullins, Jenny Strasburg, and Tom McGinty, "Stock Surge Linked to Lobbyist
Trading in Health-Care Shares Soared After a Research Firm's Report About a Coming Policy Change," *The Wall Street Journal*, April 17, 2013
http://www.wsj.com/news/articles/SB10001424127887324345804578427102504475618

Alicia Mundy and Brody Mullins, "Tip Puts Lobbyist's Career on Hold," *The Wall Street Journal*, May 20, 2013, http://

www.wsj.com/articles/SB1000142412788732346370457 84
93101424792638

Brody Mullins, Jean Eaglesham, and Devlin Barrett, "Probe of How U.S. Agency's Medicare Move Reached Investors Hits Wall," *The Wall Street Journal,* November 21, 2013, http://www.wsj.com/articles/SB100014240527023046071045792 10320473074320

Brody Mullins and Andrew Ackerman, "House Panel Is Subpoenaed as Trading Probe Heats Up Prosecutors Gathering Evidence for Grand Jury in Centers for Medicare and Medicaid Services Leak Case," *The Wall Street Journal,* June 18, 2014, http://www.wsj.com/articles/prosecutors-gathering-evidence-for-grand-jury-in-cms-leak-case-1403130561

Jia Lynn Yang and Jerry Markon, "Greenberg Traurig law firm at the center of 'political intelligence' case," *The Washington Post,* May 6, 2013, http://www.washingtonpost.com/business/economy/greenberg-traurig-law-firm-at-the-center-of-political-intelligence-case/2013/05/06/7e0b01fa-b437-11e2-bbf2-a6f9e9d79e19_story.html

Jia Lynn Yang, Tom Hamburger, and Dina ElBoghdady, "How 'political intelligence' can come from Congress itself," *The Washington Post*, May 6, 2013, http://www. washingtonpost.com/business/economy/how-political-intelligence-can-come-from-congress-itself/2013/05/06/a2998e4c-b68a-11e2-b94c-b684dda07add_story.html

Tom Hamburger and Dina ElBoghdady, "Hundreds in government had advance word of Medicare action at heart of trading-spike probe," *The Washington Post*, June 9, 2013, http://www.washingtonpost.com/politics/hundreds-in-government-had-advance-word-of-medicare-action-at-heart-of-trading-spike-probe/2013/06/09/044944d0-cec7-11e2-8845-d970ccb04497_story.html

Tom Hamburger and Dina ElBoghdady, "SEC subpoenas 'political intelligence' firms in a case of leaked information," *The Washington Post*, May 1, 2013, http://www.washingtonpost. com/business/economy/sec-issues-subpoenas-to-political-intelligence-firms-connected-to-leaked-information/201 3/05/01/43121794-b290-11e2-bbf2-a6f9e9d79e19_story. html

Tom Hamburger and Dina ElBoghdady, "Timing of political intelligence probed," *The Washington Post*, May 3, 2013, http://www.washingtonpost.com/politics/timing-of-polit-ical-intelligence-probed/2013/05/03/9128c776-b429-11e2-bbf2-a6f9e9d79e19_story.html

Brody Mullins, Jean Eaglesham, and Devlin Barrett, "Probe of How U.S. Agency's Medicare Move Reached Investors Hits Wall Incident Has Put Spotlight on Political-Intelligence Business in Washington," *The Wall Street Journal,* November 21, 2013, http://www.wsj.com/articles/SB1000142405270 2304607104579210320473074320

Brody Mullins and Tom McGinty, "SEC Broadens Its Probe of 'Political Intelligence'," *The Wall Street Journal,* May 3, 2013, http://www.wsj.com/articles/SB10001424127887324582004578461492267383464

You have the right to remain silent

Dan Dipietro, "The Dos and Don'ts of Social Media Disclosure," *Wall Street Journal,* October 22, 2013, http://blogs.wsj.com/riskandcompliance/2013/10/22/the-dos-and-donts-of-social-media-disclosure/

Liz Rappaport and Katy Burne, "Goldman Looks to Ban Some Chat Services Used by Traders," *Wall Street Journal,* January

23, 2014, http://www.wsj.com/articles/SB1000142405270 2304856504579337063884425156

Susan M. Heathfield, "Internet and Email Policy," *About Money,* http://humanresources.about.com/od/policiesand samples1/a/email_policy.htm

Ben Dipietro, "Laws Try to Resolve Employer-Employee Social Media Conflicts," *Wall Street Journal,* May 28, 2015, http://blogs.wsj.com/riskandcompliance/2015/05/28/laws-try-to-resolve-employer-employee-social-media-conflicts/

Erica Jones, "Axed White House Staffer Jofi Joseph Issues Apology for 'Inappropriate' Tweets" *NBCWashington. com,* October 23, 2013, http://www.nbcwashington.com/news/local/Jofi-Joseph-White-House-Staffer-Fired-for-Tweets-228905711.html

Glenn Thrush, "NSC aide admits Twitter attack on White House," *Politico 44,* October 22, 2013, http://www.politico.com/politico44/2013/10/nsc-aide-admits-twitter-attack-on-white-house-175722.html

Jackie Calmes, "White House Official on National Security Is Fired After Twitter Posts Are Unmasked," *New York*

Times Online, October 23, 2013, http://www.nytimes.com/2013/10/24/us/secret-white-house-tweeter-and-national-security-council-official-loses-job.html?_r=0

Neal Colgrass, "Ex-CFO who slammed Chick-fil-A now on foodstamps," *Newser,* March 28, 2015, http://www.newser.com/story/204656/ex-cfo-who-slammed-chick-fil-a-lives-on-food-stamps.html?utm_source=part&utm_medium=usatoday&utm_campaign=syn

Ken Klukowski, "NRA takes aim at Obama's anti-gun Surgeon General nominee Vivik Murthy," *Brietbart,* 19 March 2014, http://www.breitbart.com/big-government/2014/03/19/nra-takes-aim-at-vivek-murthy-obama-s-anti-gun-surgeon-general-nominee/

Jennifer Pompi, "Senate confirms Vivek Murthy, gun control advocate, as surgeon general," *The Washington Times,* Dec. 15, 2014, http://www.washingtontimes.com/news/2014/dec/15/vivek-murthy-confirmed-senate-surgeon-general/

Cheating in Congress

Marcella Bombardieri, "Harvard dean at center of e-mail controversy resigning," *Boston Globe,* May 28, 2013

https://www.bostonglobe.com/metro/2013/05/28/
harvard/2x9DGNZeQxV2kZn9Px9LrL/story.html

Martine Powers and Katherine Landergan, "Harvard details
suspensions in massive cheating scandal" *Boston Globe*,
February 2, 2013
https://www.bostonglobe.com/metro/2013/02/02/
harvard-details-suspensions-massive-cheating-
scandal/6gzGzU2WvbFG17T4kAq50L/story.html?
p1=Article_Related_Box_Article_More

Mary Carmichael, "Harvard University officials wanted to find
the source of a leaked confidential e-mail about last year's
cheating scandal," *Boston Globe*, March 12, 2013
https://www.bostonglobe.com/metro/2013/03/11/
harvard/QCueLlOPua1L6062sWFNVO/story.html?
p1=Article_Related_Box_Article

Mary Carmichael and Peter Schworm, "Secret e-mail searches
on Harvard cheating scandal broader than initially
described," *Boston Globe*, April 02, 2013
http://www.boston.com/metrodesk/2013/04/02/secret-
mail-searches-harvard-cheating-scandal-broader-than-
initially-described/Mgz0mc8hSk3IgWGjxLwsJP/story.
html

Rande Iaboni and Dana Ford, "Months after a secret e-mail search controversy at Harvard College, Evelynn M. Hammonds announced on Tuesday that she will step down as dean on July 1, according to a statement posted online," *CNN*, May 29, 2013

http://www.cnn.com/2013/05/28/us/massachusetts-harvard-dean/

Richard Perez-Pena, "Dean in E-Mail Searches Steps Down at Harvard

New York Times, MAY 28, 2013 http://www.nytimes. com/2013/05/29/education/harvard-dean-in-e-mail-controversy-to-step-down.html?_r=0&module=CloseSlid eshow&region=SlideShowTopBar&version=SlideCard-10 &action=click&contentCollection=Fashion%20%26%20 Style&pgtype=imageslideshow

J. K. Trotter, "Harvard Dean Steps Down Over Search of Faculty Email," *The Wire*, MAY 28, 2013

http://www.thewire.com/national/2013/05/ harvard-dean-steps-down-over-secret-email-search/65643/

Jena McGregory, "The Harvard email controversy," *Washington Post*, March 11, 2013
https://www.washingtonpost.com/national/on-leadership/the-harvard-email-controversy/2013/03/11/abdebb32-8a73-11e2-8d72-dc76641cb8d4_story.html

Richard Perez-Pena and Jess Bidgoodmarch, "Harvard Explains Why Staff E-Mails Were Searched," *The New York Times*, March 11, 2013
http://www.nytimes.com/2013/03/12/education/harvard-search-e-mail-accounts.html?_r=1

Richard Perez-Pena, "Harvard Search of E-Mail Stuns Its Faculty Members," *The New York Times*, March 10, 2013
http://www.nytimes.com/2013/03/11/us/harvard-e-mail-search-stuns-faculty-members.html

Nikita Kansra and Samuel Y. Weinstock, "Administrators Secretly Searched Resident Deans' Email for Cheating Scandal Leak," *The Harvard Crimson*, March 9, 2013
http://www.thecrimson.com/article/2013/3/9/cheating-leak-email-search/

Nicholas P. Fandos and Samuel Y. Weinstock, "Administrators' Statement on Secret Email Searches Leaves Questions Unanswered," *The Harvard Crimson*, March 11, 2013
http://www.thecrimson.com/article/2013/3/11/admins-email-statement/?page=1

Alexander Koenig and Robert S. Samuels, "Football Bracing for Lineup Changes Following Government 1310 Incident," *The Harvard Crimson*, September 10, 2012
http://www.thecrimson.com/article/2012/9/10/football-cheating-scandal/

Rebecca D. Robbins, "Cheating Scandal To Be Reviewed Case-by-Case," *The Harvard Crimson*, September 11, 2012
http://www.thecrimson.com/article/2012/9/11/cheating-students-judged-individually/

"I should have never have sent them."

Securities and Exchange Commission, Plaintiff – against-Steven H. Davis, Stephen Dicarmine, Joel Sanders, Francis Canellas, Thomas Mulligan, CV-14 (1528) Complaint, https://s3.amazonaws.com/s3.documentcloud.org/documents/1063614/s-e-c-complaint-against-ex-leaders-of-law-firm.pdf

James B. Stewart, "The Collapse" *The New Yorker,* October, 14, 2013

http://www.newyorker.com/magazine/2013/10/14/the-collapse-2

Matthew Goldstein, "Trial Opens in Collapse of Dewey & LeBoeuf Firm," *The New York Times,* May 26, 2015, http://www.nytimes.com/2015/05/27/business/dealbook/trial-opens-in-collapse-of-dewey-leboeuf-firm.html?_r=0

Matthew Goldstein, "Dewey & LeBoeuf Trial Is Expected to Be Lengthy," *The New York Times,* May 26, 2015, http://www.nytimes.com/2015/04/27/business/dealbook/dewey-leboeuf-trial-is-expected-to-be-lengthy.html

Sara Randazzo, "Things to Know About the Dewey & LeBoeuf Trial," *The Wall Street Journal,* May 22, 2015, http://blogs.wsj.com/briefly/2015/05/22/5-to-know-about-the-dewey-leboeuf-criminal-trial/

Peter Lattman and Michael J. De La Merced, "A Prominent Bankruptcy Lawyer Now Ministers to His Firm," *The New York Times,* April 20, 2012, http://dealbook.nytimes.com/2012/04/20/a-prominent-bankruptcy-lawyer-now-ministers-to-his-firm/

Jennifer Smith and Ashby Jones, "Fallen Law Firm's Leaders Are Charged With Fraud," *The Wall Street Journal*, March 6, 2015, http://www.wsj.com/articles/SB1000142405270230 4554004579423082266343204

Sara Randazzo, "Emails to Play Key Role in Dewey & LeBoeuf Trial," *The Wall Street Journal*, May 25, 2015, http://www.wsj.com/articles/emails-to-play-key-role-in-dewey-leboeuf-trial-1432546382

Matthew Goldstein and Ben Protess, "Criminal Charges Expected for 3 Former Dewey & LeBoeuf Executives" *The Wall Street Journal*, March 5, 2014, http://dealbook.nytimes.com/2014/03/05/top-former-dewey-leboeuf-executives-said-to-face-charges/

Peter Lattman, "Dewey's Bienenstock Discusses Law Firm's Demise," *The New York Times*, May 14, 2012, http://dealbook.nytimes.com/2012/05/14/deweys-bienenstock-discusses-law-firms-demise/

Peter Lattman, "Defections Continue at Dewey & LeBoeuf," *The New York Times*, April 4, 2012, http://dealbook.nytimes.com/2012/04/04/dewey-leboeuf-loses-six-more-partners/

Peter Lattman, "Partner Exodus May Upend Dewey's Loans," *The New York Times,* April 18, 2012, http://query.nytimes.com/gst/fullpage.html?res=9401E5D61230F93BA25757C0A9649D8B63

Stewart Bishop, "Fake Income' Email Shows No Fraud, Dewey CFO Contends" *Law 360,* May 27 2015 http://www.law360.com/articles/660715/-fake-income-email-shows-no-fraud-dewey-cfo-contends

ACKNOWLEDGMENTS

I am deeply appreciative to those who helped in the editing of this book.

Casey Robinson, Ph.D.
Steve Styers, mountaineer extraordinaire
Kelly Robinson, my *paison*

ABOUT THE AUTHOR

Kent Robinson lives in St. Louis, Missouri with his wife and three children. He has worked since 2002 in the field of genetic diagnostics and the design and execution of clinical trials in oncology.  He enjoys spending time with his family, swimming, and hiking.

He has a doctorate in biochemistry and molecular biology and an MBA. His previous work was published in the journals of *Biochimica et Biophysica Acta, The Journal of Neurochemistry, Proceedings of the American Association for Cancer Research,* and other scientific journals.

To learn more please go to www.kentalanrobinson. com.